ONE DAY IN JULY

ONE DAY IN JULY

Experiencing 7/7

John Tulloch

Survivor of the Edgware Road Bomb

LITTLE, BROWN

£14·99

LITTLE, BROWN

First published in Great Britain in 2006 by Little, Brown

Copyright © John Tulloch 2006

The right of John Tulloch to be identified as the Author of this work has been asserted by him in accordance with the Copyrights, Designs and Patents Act 1988.

The publisher is grateful for permission to reproduce extracts from *Saturday* by Ian McEwan, published by Jonathan Cape, reprinted by permission of The Random House Group Ltd; and from the radio programme *London Bombings – The Way Forward*, courtesy of BBC Radio Five Live and Unique.

A CIP catalogue record for this book is available from the British Library.

Hardback ISBN-13: 978-0-316-02958-2
Hardback ISBN-10: 0-316-02958-0
C format ISBN-13: 978-0-316-02988-9
C format ISBN-10: 0-316-02988-2

Typeset in Baskerville by M Rules
Printed and bound in Great Britain by
Clays Ltd, St Ives plc

Little, Brown Book Group
Brettenham House
Lancaster Place
London WC2E 7EN

A member of the Hachette Livre Group of Companies

www.littlebrown.co.uk

To all victims of the 'war on terror'

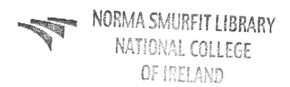

Contents

One day in July I stepped off a London street into Euston Square Underground Station. I slowed my walk towards the copies of Metro, *the free morning newspaper, and then headed on down to the platform as quickly as I could. It was rush hour; it was crowded. As I approached the platform, I could tell that I had just missed a train. People were pouring towards me up the stairs, away from the tracks. Then I looked up at the board and felt some relief. I should make it to Paddington in time for the 9.15 a.m. train after all. It was 8.46. Another Circle Line train was due in just one minute.*

One day in July a young Brazilian electrician took a bus from Tulse Hill in south-east London to Stockwell. He entered the Underground station and he also paused to pick up a copy of Metro. *He went through the barriers with his Travelcard, and then calmly down the escalators towards the platform. Near the bottom he could hear a train was approaching and, anxious to reach it, he started to run on to the platform. Behind him, his pursuers, whom he was completely unaware of at the time, picked up their speed and ran towards him.*

These incidents exist as emotional parallels for me. Both were directly connected to extreme acts of terrorist violence the like of which London had never before experienced. Both began at the station with the automatic, everyday action of moving to the free newspaper. Both involved a last-minute rush to the platform to reach a train. But there is also a world of difference between them. The experience of the Brazilian will always be unknowable. He died horribly on that train with several point-blank shots to the head, a victim of a policy that was supposedly designed to protect him. My experience of the London bombings – the massive explosion just outside Edgware Road Station, the aftermath, the days and months spent coming to terms with what happened – will follow in the pages of this book.

I hope to put de Menezes' picture and mine in the wider context of the fears and threats we all face: of further terrorism, and of ongoing danger not only to each of us personally and our everyday lives but to our political systems via the images that the media construct out of us. Because, let's make no bones about it, democracy is severely threatened – and not just by the terrorists themselves, but by the kind of action that killed Jean Charles de Menezes, and some of the reactions in the media to his death.

Yet this book is also about other, more positive forces at work in society, forces that should give us cause for great optimism. It is about the work of so many people in the streets and hospitals of London on 7 July, people who live every day by the values that our politicians like to talk about; it's about the many communicators in the newspapers, media, theatre and arts who insist, so rightly, on offering alternative viewpoints on terror and democracy, and who ask egalitarian, and thus civilised, questions, rather than impose answers using the spin that has become customary among politicians.

Inevitably, though, this will be mainly my story. What happened to me on 7 July was totally unexpected, dramatic and unpleasant. I want to tell you about it, partly because sitting here now, reliving it helps me to come to terms with it; and partly because it is not to be shied away from. It happened. It happened for a whole range of reasons. But it should not be forgotten.

Preface

The Circle Line train pulled in. I toyed with getting into the first carriage because I could see the second was crowded. But I saw just one vacant seat in carriage two, next to the end of a bench seat along the wall between two double doors. There was a very big guy in the next seat, sort of spilling over into what seemed too narrow a space for me and my bags. Other people were obviously thinking the same thing and not taking the seat. You make split decisions. I didn't have time now to pull my bags back to the first carriage, so I plunged in and squeezed into the gap, with my roller case tight against my legs. My laptop bag was on my knees and my black cabin bag was on top of that. We set off, typically packed in, towards Paddington.

I'm not sure where they got in, but after a while I was aware of two American voices, students I thought, in the two seats next to me on my left, with the big man still on my right. They were talking like people who knew each other well. I didn't listen particularly to what they were saying, but their cheerful voices were a ray of pleasure in that humourless, everyday dash we all do to work each morning.

Then, at Edgware Road Station, the carriage seemed to empty of about half its passengers. I was surprised because that tends to happen at Paddington, not the stop before. But it suited me because all the people in the aisle got out or found seats, and even better, the large man next to me left the train.

I was looking to breathe out even before that. Just before my man got out, the guy opposite him got up too and I was already eyeing his seat and wondering whether it was worth the effort of moving all my bags across. I had been looking across the carriage just before this at a kind of tweedy, lugubrious but gentle-looking man standing in the double doorway opposite the American women. He looked a bit lonely, a bit out of place. I took him for a rambler caught up in the rush-hour Tube. He certainly wasn't pushy, because, as I was wondering about lurching with my bags across the carriage to the vacant seat, he was looking around at everyone, as though keen not to take a seat anyone else might want. I didn't move, though, and he took that seat. Then the big man next to me got up, so I shifted along into his seat. I moved my roller case to the right, slightly into the double doorway now next to me, dumped my cabin bag on the seat I'd just vacated between me and the two Americans, and kept the laptop on my knees.

We rolled out of Edgware Road, with me and the lugubrious man sitting facing each other, and me breathing easier because I had more space and because the train sometimes stops for ages at Edgware Road and this time it didn't. I was anxious about getting my connecting Cardiff train at 9.15, and only about fifty metres into the tunnel from Edgware Road I began to push down on the seat with my hands to stand up, get my bags organised and be ready for a quick exit in the doorway. But it was still only 8.56 a.m. by my watch, so I eased back into the seat because it was too early to get up.

That action saved my life because I was now sitting only three feet from the suicide bomber standing in that doorway. Had I been standing, there would have been nothing but air between me and the bomb. And about three seconds later, it happened.

People talk about Ground Zero in New York after 9/11. They do that, I suppose, because everything that was material, everything that existed – the twin towers – was reduced to dust and rubble; a move from civilisation via terror to *nihil*, nothing. But there is another way in which I came to think of that destroyed carriage of the Circle Line train on 7/7 as 'underground zero', as one newspaper called it. It wasn't just the physical apparatus of London's transport technology that was brought to nothing that day. It was also my own everyday actions, plans and preconceptions. My daily narrative was brought to nothing, my plans to write a research proposal and a paper on risk that day and the next just wasted away, and were replaced by a zero condition – where I had no idea what had happened or what my purpose now was.

In the days after the attacks I was in terrible pain. I suffered from head injuries, concussion and such a feeling of helplessness that I felt desperate at night if I couldn't touch and feel the urine bottle I knew I would need. Often I wondered how I would turn to use it without severe pain since I couldn't sit; and I was tortured by the thought of new waves of pain through my head as I turned to one side or vomited again and again in the little crescent-shaped bowl beside my hospital bed.

What happened to me as a result of the bombing is just one part of the story. I am an academic who works in the area of media and risk and so my natural take, soon after the explosion as well as now, was on how the media were using my experience, particularly the images of me as a concussed victim outside Edgware Road Station and in my hospital bed. How did they mould me and my experience to fit into place for their reporting?

Only a few months before 7 July I was saying in a keynote address at a major conference on risk that academics should broaden their focus from the current preoccupation with science and risk, to start looking at the issue of the new 'humanitarian' wars like Kosovo, Afghanistan and Iraq, and to examine the implications of these wars at home. Indeed, I was so keen to make the point that I had actually changed the subject of my paper from 'risk and everyday life' (which I had been asked to do) to one on media imaging of contemporary warfare. And then, on 7 July and the days following it, the 'humanitarian' Iraq war literally exploded in my face, in my eyes, in my ears and, as I lay in hospital, in my thoughts and feelings.

When I gave that paper I could have had no idea that I would soon be appearing on the front pages of newspapers around the world, not for my ideas about risk but because of my experience of it – that now familiar image of me much damaged by the terrorist attack. The result was galvanising as well as crippling. The London bombs and their aftermath reinforced those earlier thoughts I'd had, and led them in different directions. For weeks after the bombings, I couldn't read much, but I could peruse newspapers as they began to tell the awful stories of those who died, and the emerging tales of the suicide bombers themselves. The pain I was in as I looked at those images and those accounts of 7 July led me to connect strongly with others who had suffered far more than I had.

But – and maybe it was because of that keynote speech I'd given – I had fearful fantasies of something else: what if all that wonderful support I was getting in the hospital suddenly vanished, as had happened to uncounted people in Fallujah? Worse still, what if the 'bad guys' came back and beat up my pulverised body some more, as had happened at Abu Ghraib? It was only because I was in so much pain that I could even have such thoughts. But have them I surely did, even through the genuine smiles of the nurses who came to help me through the day. It was a kind of recurring nightmare during those first few days after the bombings.

Then as friends started to bring newspapers in, something else took the place of these thoughts. I began to perceive how the images of the victims of 7 July, the ones who had walked out alive, were being used. Not many survivors from carriage two of the Circle Line train at Edgware Road came walking out. Seven people died in it and others were horribly injured, but Davinia Turrell and I came stumbling on to the street, and her image and mine both appeared immediately across the world, and then reappeared frequently over the next couple of months, becoming iconic representations of what had happened.

The photographs of us told of the stark horror of the attack. Both pictures were used internationally as the backdrop to television newsreaders telling of the bombings, and both appeared on the same page of the 8 July issue of the *Independent* under the headings 'A severely injured woman is escorted away from Edgware Road Tube station' and 'An injured passenger is helped by ambulance staff at Edgware Road'.

The media coverage of human catastrophe – whether major bush fires in Australia or terrorist bombings in London – tends always to follow the same mini-narrative. First come stories and pictures of the shock of the disaster and the heroic struggles by professionals to contain it. This happens on the first day or two of coverage after the event. Then there is talk of the dreadful loss of life, of individual tragedies, of 'ifs' and 'buts' and 'onlys' as the coincidence of horror and sorrow. And then, soon after, the cycle of blame begins. Who was responsible? Where are they now? Where are they from? What should be done to prevent this from ever happening again? Jean Charles de Menezes died as a result of that particular discourse of blame.

So the early images of Davinia and myself belonged to a tried and tested 'heroic' first stage: that of the victims and their helpers. It is no coincidence, then, that the pictures of Davinia always included in close-up the purposeful young man Paul Dadge helping her, guiding her to safety. Similarly, all the many slightly different shots that I saw of me emerging at Edgware Road showed me surrounded by police and emergency services. The big photograph in the *Sydney Morning Herald* of me with a female emergency worker helping me by arranging a purple

blanket over my right shoulder and arm, a frowning and concerned ambulance man just behind me and another female
medic in a white coat holding my left arm and carrying my one
surviving travel bag over her shoulder, belonged to that genre.

But as iconic images, the photographs of Davinia and myself
were to become rather different. The initial photographs of me,
as I first experienced them, emphasised the blood and gore of
the event. They represented the publicly acceptable face of the
carnage that some of those same helpers must have seen inside
carriage two of the train. In the photo, my entire face is so covered and encrusted with blood and burns that some people who
knew me well didn't recognise me. My eyes are swollen and
unfocused through concussion; my mouth is set in a line of pain;
my shrapnel-damaged nose looks like some craggy impastoed
object in a late self-portrait by Rembrandt. My head (which sustained the worst damage) is partially covered by an improvised
bandage, with ragged blue and yellow cloth hanging down my
face and exposed chest. Above the bandage you can see my
forehead covered in debris; below it layers of my ruined clothing, my damaged hands and, hanging there, a prominent label
saying, 'PRIORITY 3'. This seemed an image of complete
helplessness, which Liz, my upset colleague at Brunel
University, told me brought to mind those awful Nazi concen-
tration camp images of cowed people with labels hanging off
them. The detritus of terror.

Davinia's images, as I first saw them, were different for two
reasons. The figure of Davinia's helper, with his clean, white-
jacketed arms and blue, plastic-gloved hands placed protectively
around her, is much more active than my helpers as he leans not
only over her but into the camera, driving forwards deter-
minedly, bringing her out of the horror and into civilised safety.
The second difference is the striking, white surgical mask that
Davinia is holding to her face with both her hands. Whereas my
hands are seen bandaged, damaged, burnt and helpless,

Davinia's are active, holding up her mask and co-ordinating with the drive of her helper. In this image the mask signifies two other things. It hides (but makes us imagine) the damage to her face; and, together with the dynamic action of the photo in general, it emphasises the drama of the rescue, in contrast to the documentary-style flatness of the images of me as victim.

Behind these images were two people who had just been through the worst experience of their lives. That experience could not, no matter how hard the newspapers tried, be represented by the pictures that appeared on their front pages. It was an experience that was part of a wider narrative, because, as with all major events, everybody has a story about where they were or what they were doing when the bombs went off.

For me, it began when I finished the last sip of my morning cup of coffee and headed out of the front door of my friend Janet's flat in Camden Town with my bags, ready for the walk to the Tube. I don't know where it will end. But this book is a pathway, which will talk about the images, words and performances I saw in the months spent rebuilding my physical, psychological and intellectual identities after 7/7. In those highways and byways I found many encouraging things about our democracy, all differing from the routine rhetoric we get from politicians about democracy, freedom and terror.

ONE

7 July: 'The Wrong Place at the Wrong Time'

Everyone injured or bereaved by the 7/7 explosions will have had the phrase running around their own or their comforters' thoughts: 'the wrong place at the wrong time for me/for my loved one'. And two weeks after the bombings, the media used it consistently about the killing of the Brazilian man, Jean Charles de Menezes. It is true, of course, but also a cliché and not much to work back from, because it underplays our freedom to make everyday decisions about where we are and when.

We who experienced the explosions had made active choices to be doing what we were doing at the time of the terrorist attacks. We were also subject to a wide range of contexts determining why we were there, and what happened to us there. Some of those contexts are very cruel. However, not all of them were, and to forget the loving ones, the ties of friendship and professionalism, the loyalties, preoccupations, obsessions and coincidences that put us in 'the wrong place at the wrong time' is to do more of the terrorists' work for them. It is those personal choices, actions and contexts that make up the values that our politicians talk so much about defending, but that we, the different publics, the citizens, the civil society, live every day, and lived especially vividly on 7 July 2005.

I want to start with my own preoccupations that day. I know this kind of recall has been an important therapy to those injured or bereaved that I have spoken with, or have heard speak in the media. And it also has been crucial to my forming an initial understanding of what happened.

When you encounter a shocking, near-death experience like 7/7, many of the circumstantial details around the bombing etch themselves for ever, replaying many times a day, month after month. Other details get lost in the shock and the trauma. In my case the concussion that was evident in the first photographs of me at Edgware Road still lingers even as I write this. Some of the missing details are brought back by those who were close to you that day. Others are recalled after seeing images or hearing other people's stories in the media. Post-trauma stress psychologists encourage victims to fill out diaries in order to bring a sense of narrative control to what otherwise is a horrendously vulnerable experience, living on in dreadful flashbacks after the bomb.

For me there is more to it than that, valuable therapy though it is. It is not so much the remembering and archiving of every detail, action and context around that experience that matters to me, but rather a new emotional engagement with what happened. I have had plenty of time to revisit that day, and not just through my own memory but through that of people who came very close to me on 7 July itself and the following days, and through the many public voices that have since expressed their own thoughts and emotions.

Early morning

So why was I at the wrong place at the wrong time? Normally – because I work on a 70 per cent research contract and live in

Cardiff – I would have travelled home on Wednesday evening, 6 July, and so would not have been in London the following morning. However, the next Tuesday, 12 July, was the annual degree presentation for our School of Social Sciences and Law at Brunel University – it would be my job to announce the Ph.D. graduates that afternoon – and there had been a special training session for us on the Wednesday evening. So I had stayed in London that night.

I might have set out for Cardiff earlier on 7 July if I had been staying in the comfortable small flat I rent from my friends John and Maire, very near Tavistock Square, where a bus was blown up that morning, and under which a Piccadilly Line Tube train was destroyed. However, one of John and Maire's daughters had asked to use the flat during July and August. So on the night of 6 July I was staying at the Camden flat of my friend Janet, and requiring a start-off to Cardiff from the same Tube station I would have used if I had been staying near Tavistock Square: Euston Square.

Same Tube station but almost certainly a later starting point that morning, because my London flat experience was more monastic, whereas Janet's flat is a thriving hub of family, friends and generosity, and I was sinking into it that morning. I reckoned that the latest time I could afford to get back to Cardiff was about midday. I had to fix up Heather, who had been looking after my Cardiff flat while I had been away a month in Australia, and who was leaving at one o'clock; and I also had about two hours of writing to complete in Cardiff that afternoon for a research centre proposal on 'Media, Risk and Globalisation' for Brunel University. I had worked hard and long on that proposal the day before at Brunel, so I gave up the idea of getting the 8.15 a.m. from Paddington to Cardiff, and sat back to the luxury of freshly made coffee and toast at Janet's.

I was now aiming for the 9.15 a.m. out of Paddington, and I was drinking that coffee at 7.25 a.m. – precisely the time, as I learned later, that the four terrorist bombers were captured on CCTV entering Luton Station. It amazed me later how far they travelled and how little I did except talk, eat toast and drink coffee between then and when we met at 8.56 a.m.

My walk from Janet's flat to Euston Square Station would normally have taken about ten minutes. But that day I had three bags: my long-haul flight luggage from Australia the previous weekend. Janet offered to help me with my roller case to the Tube station, and so it was that we were approaching Euston Square when I was stopped by a confused visitor trying to find an address in Camden. I had no idea where it was, but Janet did, and with a librarian's meticulousness and the same generosity that brought her out to pull my bag to the station, she seemed to spend a very long time answering the lady's questions. It was now about 8.35 a.m., and I was worrying about missing my Cardiff train from Paddington. So I did that usual trick of walking ahead a few paces, stopping, looking back, and eventually walking back to them, still conversing, before the lady was finally satisfied, and we set off for the last few minutes to Euston Square.

At the station, now with all three bags, I started moving faster, pausing for the 'London Olympic Victory' *Metro*, but deciding I was too encumbered and too short of time. I bought my ticket, struggled through the barrier with my bags and manhandled them down the two flights of stairs to the westbound platform. You always know at Euston Square whether you have missed a train, because there are people pouring up the steps towards you. I hurried on and got to the platform to see a Paddington train just pulling out.

I looked up at the indicator board and was relieved to see that a Circle Line train for Paddington was due in just one minute. I positioned myself at the top end of the platform. I wanted to get in the second carriage because at Paddington that stops opposite the platform exit, which always gets logjammed in peak periods. To get out fast saves you the crucial minutes to maybe catch that other train.

In less than a minute the train arrived. The second carriage was packed but as I could see one spare seat I decided to go for it. I squeezed into the seat next to the large man and pulled my bags around me. When he got out at Edgware Road, three stops later, I moved across to his seat at the end of the row. As passengers got off and on, the mournful-looking man that had been standing in the double doorway moved to sit in the seat opposite me. The train set off again. I listened to the voices of the two American women as they talked on my left. My stop was next and I thought about getting up to stand ready in the doorway. I looked at my watch: it was 8.56 a.m.

In the next instant there exploded suddenly into my vision a strange and uncomfortable image of that carriage. Everything turned a horrible, urine-coloured yellow. The carriage seemed to be distorting, being pulled and displaced as though it were a flat, rubberised photograph that someone was yanking at the sides. I heard no sound. (I read three days later that experienced soldiers tell you if you don't hear the sound of an explosion you are probably about to die.) I don't remember seeing anything being detached and flying around: bodies, parts of seats, my own bags. It all seemed still one connected image, but deconstructed by distortion and stretching. I do remember a very disagreeable feeling, where everything was wrong, out of phase, inconvenient and, in that instant, unknowable.

Next I was on my back, slumped on a wrecked seat, my spectacles blown away, blood all over my face and head. It was dark in the carriage. There was blood everywhere. The support pole at the end of the bench seat was at an extreme angle over me, and had probably caused the damage to my head. But at that moment, at underground zero, I wasn't connecting such things. I knew something bad had happened to me, and I remembered those two fresh American voices near me minutes before. I rolled to my left to ask them for help – to help me find my glasses so I could see. I think I even began to speak to them. But then I saw them, one slumped on the seat, the other on the floor, both in a terrible way and bleeding. Only then did it occur to me that something bad had happened to everybody.

There is a strange and embarrassing sense of solipsism about this, which I talked over with my Australian social worker Lou when she visited me two weeks later. Lou had been in contact with the victims of the first Bali bombing, and explained that in a near-death situation the body moves quickly into survival mode, generating huge amounts of adrenalin that give us the energy to fight (to protect ourselves from danger) or flight (away from trouble). So, Lou said, that 'Me, Me' focus at the beginning was programmed and normal, and it certainly helps explain what happened next. Despite the considerable pain in my head, and my extreme shock at seeing the two badly injured women next to me, something brought my attention back to the good parts of my body. My feet and legs felt really good, and I was determined to try them out. So the next thing, I was on my feet, going looking for my cases and glasses.

With my impaired vision – no glasses, one eye completely closed and the other half-closed – I couldn't see much in the dark and the smoke. I could see that there was considerable damage to the floor of the carriage in front and, to my right, some sort of concave shape to the floor, and in that lay a man's body. I worried instantly for the man opposite, but I'm squeamish at the best of times and knew that looking at him wouldn't help either of us. Besides which, I was in survival mode, the only person on his feet in the carriage, and heading off to look for my bags.

Those bags had almost certainly saved my legs, especially the roller case, which was between me and the bomb. (It was returned to me in a shocking condition a couple of months later by the bomb squad. Likewise the laptop and its case. They all looked, in the words of the bomb squad detective, as if he had taken to them with a high-powered gun.) The case and my laptop would be in tatters, and at the time covered in blood and no doubt body parts. But they were not my body parts, which were driving me across that wrecked carriage. The only shrapnel in my legs was in my thigh. Otherwise my feet and legs were in fine shape, and the strong shoes I was wearing bore only a few traces of shrapnel in the right toe.

However, at the time I wasn't thinking about my bags in this way. I had no idea what had happened to any of us. I was in a determined mode, pleased to be looking after myself again, and able to walk across the carriage and sit on the burned seat opposite. That was the significance, I think, of my obsession with retrieving my bags and glasses. It was my reaction to extreme threat, and it was about the only bit of knowledge or narrative thread I had in my moment-by-moment life then.

There was, though, perhaps one other factor about my 'find the bags' obsession just then: a shard of memory that my cabin bag contained my computer memory stick, with not only my research for two full years on it but also a Ph.D. report for a Colombian student at the University of Ulster whom I was supposed to be examining in two weeks' time. If both my cabin bag containing the memory stick and the laptop were lost, all was lost of my everyday professional life.

I can't now remember whether I thought about those things then. I certainly did an hour or two later when I was struggling to hold on to my one remaining bag in the ambulance and the hospital. Indeed, my Viennese friends Gunhild and Gerhard, who visited me in hospital on 9 July, said I never stopped talking about the Ph.D. report contained in it. Yet I'm inclined to think that my obsession with it in the minutes after the explosion was more basically chemical, adrenalin-driven, and I couldn't help feeling, *Isn't it great, I survived this and I can walk.*

I'm sure that mood would not have lasted long, but I then got very lucky indeed. Having crossed the carriage diagonally to the bench seat opposite, I was now looking straight across and beyond the two injured American women, and I saw for the first time another train next to ours. It was a surreal image of contrasts. The other train looked whole; ours was wrecked. The other train was lit up; ours was dark and in smoky gloom. The other train had people all on their feet, scrabbling silhouettes at doors and windows. Our carriage seemed to have just me on my feet, with everyone else silently spreadeagled or slumped and moaning in pain, only too solidly material and twisted, unlike the shadows of the next carriage. The two trains seemed wholly incommensurate, not of the same system, visually discordant with each other. But that second train did enable me to begin to fill in my new everyday life from ground zero. I thought then we had been in a train crash.

Then – the good luck – out of that train figures came. And one was Wing Commander Craig Staniforth. I seem to remember them climbing in over the remains of a wrecked door, but Craig assures me that there were no doors, and that he had to jump from his lit train into the cave-like dark and smoke of my carriage. Craig is actually the head of a medical support team at RAF Lyneham, and was on his way to a meeting in London when his train, travelling in the opposite direction, ran into the doors and other debris of my train. He told me later that it took him about fifteen minutes to realise there *was* another train in all that chaos, and to be alerted by a man bleeding profusely from the face that there were people in it urgently in need of help. Craig had no equipment with him, and his training would have urged extreme caution in making the decision to jump across live rails into complete uncertainty.

Yet Craig did jump, and discovered me, among the dead and grievously injured. As he told Radio Five Live:

That's when I saw you, and you were just standing there, looking for something. And I couldn't see anything because it was dark. But I could see that you had got this rather horrendous head injury . . . So the first thing I did was the basic simple checks of, 'Right, can you breathe, can you hear me?' which of course was the other problem, because you couldn't hear me that well. I said, 'How is your body, limbs, legs, arms? Is there any bleeding elsewhere? Any other injuries as far as you are aware?' which you managed to answer . . . and say 'No'. I soon became aware that the main problem here was your head injury, because I couldn't see what the real problem was. All I could see was this mass of blood and everything else.

Craig's first task was to estimate the stability of my condition, given the head wounds he could see. If he had been able to see my eyes he could have assessed me more quickly. However, he had no torch (he now carries one everywhere with him), and my eyes were almost closed anyway. He had to assess me by asking questions. Here he met an obstacle. I don't remember this at all, but Craig tells me that my first response (after telling him my name and what my job was) was to say that I wanted to lie down and sleep, and to ask could he go find my bags and glasses? It seems that with the arrival of Craig my body and mind switched instantly from heroic-survivor to victim mode. I told him about my cabin bag with the memory stick. It was a small black bag with a red book in the side pocket. He remembers:

Initially one of your biggest concerns to me, believe it or not . . . was you . . . kept going on about your glasses. And the other thing as well you desperately wanted me to find was your baggage. Because your glasses were broke that was a bit of a godsend because you couldn't see the whole situation. But I thought I've got to find you something . . . then you would concentrate on what I wanted to talk about . . . I could see this bag underneath a couple of the bodies, so I had to move the bodies to get the bag . . . In the military certainly we're taught that you don't do that because of secondary devices and this sort of thing. But the change in person to you once I found your bag was absolutely amazing. You didn't bother about your glasses any more. You didn't ask me any questions about your luggage. You just held on to your bag. It was as though you had got something, you had retrieved something from the incident. That was amazing how you turned. And I'll be totally honest with you, at one stage I couldn't believe that you and I were sitting in such an awful situation but were like two guys on a park bench, discussing the future of my daughter's career and your sons'. But hey, it worked, because while you were talking I was monitoring you constantly. I could tell if you could understand what I was saying, etc., etc. Although I couldn't see anything, at least I was getting feedback. And what I needed to prevent was you wanting to go to sleep, which you desperately wanted to do.

None of this was in my ground-zero cognition right then, but Craig at this point in the conversation still thought precisely and strategically. Should he be looking after bodies that might already be dead, or treat people like myself who could have died if not cared for, with high risk of coma? Craig admits now that at the time his decision to look after me made him slightly anxious and guilty. 'Am I going for the easier option here? Should I not go forward and still look for more patients that I should be probably doing cardiac massage on, or should I be tying someone's limb up? ... But in the end you have to make that decision. And I was very conscious that you had a head injury, and with a head injury you do *not* know what is going to happen. And the person has to be monitored continuously.' Then given his choice, knowing I needed constant attention, should he disturb the two bodies, a risk, and get my bag? Again he made his informed decision – and I was so lucky that he did. And once he had my attention by returning the bag, he still had to pick a conversation topic that would drill down to my very concussed attention. He had ascertained early on that I was an academic; his daughter was doing A-levels and thinking about which universities to apply to, so here was the area to catch my attention.

And he did hold my attention, so that to this day I remember the subjects that Craig's daughter is interested in, and even the names of the universities she was thinking of applying to: Exeter, Aberystwyth, Manchester, Reading. That memory detail contrasts with my remembering little or nothing of the earlier part of our conversation, and tells me that I was looking for something to pull my old story and my horrible new one together. Meanwhile Craig was busy assessing my condition. As he told me later:

> When casualties are assessed, the basic categories are as follows (the definitions could vary):
> P1 – Requires immediate life-saving skills
> P2 – Requires immediate treatment
> P3 – Requires treatment when time permits
> P1 Hold – The injuries are so great that there may be a need to deal with P1–3 in the first instance.
> In your particular case, my initial assessment of you (once I had confirmed that you could breathe and were conscious) was a P2. My main concern was that, when I started to assess other casualties, I was aware that I had left you sitting on the seat with a severe head injury, which I was unable to fully assess. On my return and after a better assessment, I realised that although I was unable to monitor your pupils due to the darkness, the secret was to keep you talking. This way I could monitor your condition by your response. What I did not want to do was let you lie down and fall asleep. I would have

then had no idea what was happening. If you had become unconscious, I then would have regraded you as a P1, severe head injury, and ensured that when medical assistance was on site you would have been seen at the earliest opportunity.

The two of us were left talking for ages, so that the time with Craig, incredibly important to me medically, also provided a vital bridge – backwards to the shards and remnants of my past, and forwards to the next stage of my story that day.

That first stage talking with Craig was absolutely crucial to me. Unlike the recent, second Bali bombing in October 2005, where the victims were often in family groups, and where survivors experienced their injuries and bereavements together immediately (as, for example, teenagers and their parents reappeared – or didn't reappear – from their different bomb experiences), the 7/7 bombing experience was much more individualised. We were by and large on our own, lone travellers, separate from each other, cut off, with our world blown away. So, for me, Craig began to repopulate my world with the interests and intentions and stories of his family and mine. This was a hugely important beginning for me in reconstructing my identity.

Security medicine

Craig Staniforth reckons that it took between three-quarters of an hour and an hour for the emergency services to reach us. He surmises that this was a responsible policy decision on the part of the police, acutely aware of the loss of emergency service lives and resources when the firemen went quickly into the World Trade Center's twin towers in New York on 9/11. If you lose your resources (and in the case of 7/7 there was also a worry about further explosions or dirty bombs or chemical warfare), you lose your power to help. This is a rationale of emergency and security retrieval and help.

Eventually the emergency services did arrive, and some emergency workers say they came before the all-clear. After all the other injured were removed, I was helped to walk through the train by Craig on one side and a paramedic on the other. As soon as I had walked through the intervening door to the third carriage I was amazed. It was empty and, to my surprise, seemed fully intact, with its seats and fittings all in their places. Given that I still thought this was a train crash, I immediately thought, If the third carriage is okay and my second carriage is so bad, what must the first carriage be like? So I was already rejigging my theory from the idea of two trains sideswiping (after seeing the second Tube train next to ours), to one of a head-on crash, and I assumed there could be no survivors in that front carriage.

It was a long stagger down the full length of that Underground train in the dark. When I got to the very back and to the little train ladder that I'd never seen before, leading from the rear door to the ground, there was another positive sight. Not only were there lots of emergency people there busy with stretchers and other support, but I could see Edgware Road Station not more than a hundred metres away, bathed in sunlight. This was a huge psychological advantage that the Edgware Road survivors had over the survivors of the deep-level Piccadilly Line bombing between King's Cross and Russell Square. There was also much more space in the wide Edgware Road tunnel for the explosion to expend itself.

Given the surface nature of our Tube line – immediately obvious even to my concussed mind – I was already beginning to puzzle over why it had taken so long for help to get to us. Still, the emergency services were a very welcome sight now, and were wonderfully friendly and efficient. I must still have been in survival mode to some extent – the adrenalin rush that Lou told me about can last for weeks – because I told the paramedics that I was perfectly able to walk across the complex web of train lines to Edgware Road Station. Sensibly, and affably, they told me they were having none of that nonsense, and got me stretchered and out of there quick-smart. They lifted me up the slope at the end of the platform, and I remember wondering whether they would have to tilt me even more up the stairs to the station entrance. It was a bizarre concern, but maybe the first hint of feeling the dreadful vertigo which I encountered briefly (and then completely forgot about for over twenty-four hours) as Craig and my emergency service helper walked me to the side entrance of the Edgware Road Marks & Spencer, where an area had been cleared for the walking wounded. From his monitoring of me in the train, Craig advised the paramedics that I was a Priority 2 and then, once he could see me properly in the daylight, a Priority 3. And so it was that the photographs of me at Edgware Road in newspapers round the world showed a label round my neck, 'PRIORITY 3'.

Craig stayed with me for quite a time at Marks & Spencer. In the travel bag he'd brought back to me was my mobile phone, and I had two important calls I wanted to make. My closest companion in Britain was Janet, whom I wanted, and needed, to tell what had happened. But I was very deaf, and Craig helped me with the call, preparing Janet for my shaken voice and advising her I was okay and not to try to come to see me until I was in hospital. The second urgent call was to my head of school's secretary. I was terribly conscious at that moment that I was not going to be able to present the Ph.D. students for their degrees the following Tuesday, and there was one concern I had in particular. During the training session the previous evening, I had been given detailed advice about how the university was going to present *in absentia* the Ph.D. to one of our students, a young Brazilian man killed tragically in a bicycle accident after he had completed his thesis. A degree presentation is an enormously complicated ceremony, timed to the second, and subject to detailed up-to-the-last-minute tinkering with the lists that presenters read out. They have to be read, of course, in the right order, matching the waiting rows of hundreds of students. The list order has to be adjusted at the last minute for unexpected absentees. In the case of our Brazilian student, it was very important to waive the timing, normally administered with military precision, so that both his brave young partner receiving the award and the entire congregation would have time to respond with dignity and inevitable emotion. But I was now not going to be there, the presentation was only four days away and a new person had to be chosen and trained for this. Again Craig helped me to make that phone call. I told Mary, the head of school's secretary, that I had been in a serious train crash. She already knew it was a terrorist attack, but wisely chose not to burden me with that.

In Marks & Spencer they bandaged my head and prepared me for transfer to hospital. At this point Craig felt it was okay for him to leave me. I asked him to give my best wishes to his daughter as he left. Then, with Craig gone, for the first time I turned to the victim sitting on the row of chairs next to me, and asked him what he thought had happened. He was the first to tell me that there had been some sort of explosion, and he had seen a crater in the ground.

I also remember an incident when I was led into an ambulance. I protested when my bag was taken from my hands (in some photographs you can see me peering with intent at the emergency service worker who has my bag on her shoulder), and carried on protesting about it as I was led out again, when the ambulance didn't go anywhere. I think there was some confusion at the time, and lots more waiting. I imagine they were still in the massive process of clearing beds at nearby St Mary's Hospital. Then, finally, I was got into another vehicle – still eyeing my bag and being reassured it was safely with me – and taken on to hospital.

My memories of this whole period are a series of discrete images: the yellowed, destabilised carriage in the explosion; lying in the dark without my glasses, covered in blood; sitting looking past the American women to the other Tube train; the 'two guys on a bench' period with Craig; my walk through undamaged carriages on the train; the view of Edgware Road Station in the sunlight; the pavement outside the station bucking and reeling beneath my feet with the first signs of vertigo; sitting making the mobile calls in Marks & Spencer with Craig beside me; my concern for my bag in the ambulances.

Likewise, I recall only discrete images about my hospital arrival. I hardly remember the short journey to the hospital, or being wheeled in there. But I vividly remember the appearance of what I call security medicine. St Mary's is one of the chosen sites for major disaster training, and had already had to deal with the Paddington rail crash a few years earlier. I was immediately impressed and comforted by the army of medical support I received instantly on arrival.

I was wheeled into a plastic cubicle in Emergency, and laid with great care on a bed. I was hurting a lot, and in complete victim mode in my head. No more walking-wounded survival heroics now. There seemed to be so many medics all looking after me personally in that cubicle. One started to sponge my blood-encrusted forehead so gently that even where the pain was worst I felt soothed. Another medic was carefully lifting my watch off my right arm, and another the watch off my left. (I always wear two watches when on long-haul flights, and was still wearing them.) Given that I had been in hospital in London briefly the previous Saturday with open wounds on my hands after treatment for a skin condition in Australia, and given that the bomb blast had made these infinitely worse, those two careful medics taking off my watches were much appreciated. Then there seemed to be another person removing my shoes, yet another my clothes, another giving me medication, and in all there seemed to me up to ten people looking after me. All were caring, careful, professional; and I have never felt so helpless but in such good company.

After that, the rest of my day is a mosaic of images with no time continuity between them. Once moved to the hospital ward, I saw a succession of specialist doctors, none of whom I could remember as they continued to see me through the following week. However, I do remember the constant questions about my name and birth date, as they checked out my head injuries with meticulous concern. I became aware, too, that different specialists were examining me for each of the big and horrible possibilities after a close-impact explosion, even though I still had no idea how close the bomb had been. So they asked me about limbs, lungs, and later I went for two skull X-rays and a brain scan. I then remember the visit of two detective constables (one of whom was tragically killed in a car accident that weekend). It was from them I learned that my experience was a terrorist attack, and that there had been others elsewhere in London.

In this way my narrative about what had happened began to shift again, enlarge just a little and leave me very anxious for more information, which nobody was giving me. Later, there was a visit by Teresa from the Australian High Commission, offering constant support, and discussing contacting my immediate family in Australia, Marian, Anton and Rowan. The news of the bombing had broken there in the evening bulletins, but it was now the middle of the night.

Then Janet and her daughter Shona visited me in the afternoon. They had walked across London from Camden Town to Paddington, with little idea of what they would find, but much more knowledge than me about what had happened. They eschewed over-serious talk for generous badinage. Shona is a

lively lady and has an acute sense of the bizarre and the aes-
thetic. She sparred across my bed with the equally amusing Irish
nurse Aidan, and she cheered me up by saying that even though
my face was pretty bad, the 'rough look' was currently cool
(actually I had no idea how bad I looked until the following
Monday).

I also have flashes of memory, throughout the afternoon, of
continually exuding glass from my body, so that the nurses had
to change the sheets regularly; and I remember slowly raising
myself for my first supper in hospital at about 6.30 p.m., and
finding a sharp chunk of glass in my underpants (my only
remaining garment), and then another in the corner of my
mouth as I took my first spoon of soup. And finally, I remember
being wheeled into the brain-scan unit at about 9 p.m. There
was a lot of concern, I think, about my brain, with all the
glass in me, and immediately after the scan they told me it was
'A-Okay!'

Seven-seven was ending for me on a real high. I had been
shaken by many things, and I was acutely conscious of what I
was already thinking of as a stripping away of my identity: first
the explosion itself, then the literal stripping of my body down
to my underpants, including taking away my so-important cabin
bag (with all its crucial contents – memory stick, house keys,
mobile, wallet) and my gold watch, which was my grandfather's
sixtieth wedding anniversary present given to me nearly fifty
years before. I pondered that lost watch as signifying over a century of family history – and my own family and close friends
were in Australia, still unaware of my predicament. On the
other hand, I had gained new friends, carers and protectors, like
Craig, or deepened relationships, as with Janet and Shona.
Above all, I had come through all the big medical checks: my
legs were strong, my lungs had not been burnt out by the explosion and my skull X-rays and brain scan were very positive. I
was allowed just one family international call by the hospital, so

I was able to ring Marian in Australia late that evening (very early morning Australian time) to tell her what had happened but that I was fine. I was just beginning to sense how lucky I'd been, and how rich life was, and I went to sleep feeling good that night.

TWO

8 July: A Royal and a Roller-Coaster

The night of 7 July was my first in hospital as a patient – ever. Nonetheless, I had gone to sleep feeling very positive, because all those major tests had come out well and I had been able to tell Marian and my sons in Australia the good news, even as I broke to them the bad news of being caught in the attack. At least it eased Anton's anxious trawling of the internet to find out if I had been involved.

Just before 7 a.m. on 8 July in St Mary's Hospital, Paddington, I opened my eyes to Aidan, the young Irish guy with the cool spiky hair, squatting beside me doing one of the nurses' regular blood-pressure checks. Even these little tests made me anxious sometimes, because I could feel the gimlet grip on my arm get tighter and tighter, often after the nurse had popped away for something, and I wondered, What if something goes wrong and it keeps on getting tighter? And no one comes back? That right arm Aidan was probing was badly bruised and burnt from the blast, so anything hurt, and my anxiety about nurses never coming back was an emerging element in an entirely new sense of physical and environmental vulnerability.

But on this particular morning, I opened my eyes to the smiling face of Aidan just inches away. With an understated, slightly mischievous grin, he said there was maybe going to be a big event that day, even a royal event. We exchanged knowing 'Oh no's!' and complicit smiles. Then I managed breakfast without vomiting, one of few like that over the next week. And then the round of endless pills and checks began.

There was a buzz in the air of the Philip Toynbee Ward, and now they were fitting me into a pair of orange pyjamas – the ones my colleagues at Brunel called my Guantánamo pyjamas when they saw the TV pictures later that day. I guessed the clean, bright pyjamas were for the royal visit – I'd heard by now it would be Prince Charles – and wondered whether they would strip them off me after he'd gone. It wasn't until a week later that my dazed, drugged brain operated well enough to work out that my nakedness up to that 8 July morning was probably more to do with all the glass still coming out of me – I wasn't going to be stripped a second time the moment Charles left the ward. Again, though, even thinking about the pyjamas was a sign of my helplessness and vulnerability, and a clinging to anything personal that I was given, after the stripping away of my clothes, watches and cabin bag.

The Prince was due at about 10 a.m., I was told, and long before that there was a gathering of hospital staff; first in two rows facing each other to the right of my bed – specialists, nurses, administrative and public relations staff, I imagined. Then, as the clock ticked towards 10.30, this welcoming performance reconfigured into a layered semi-circle more or less round the foot of my bed. It was as though they knew something about a change of plan of which I was unaware. Maybe, I thought, the late start means the visit is going to be shorter, and it's now going to be all around me in this ward. I decided there and then that I'd better have something to say.

Like Aidan, I was fighting off a grin, which in my case was all to do with an image that I had in my head from Dennis Potter's *The Singing Detective* where all the hospital specialists are gathered around Marlow's bed, and then break into that brilliant, subversive 'Dem Bones' number. My damaged hands – the wounds from treatment for psoriasis now covered over by wounds from the explosion – gave me an affinity with Potter's bedridden hero. But anyway it was all right to smile, I thought, because I'm *alive* and my legs work, and I've passed all the hospital tests, even if my head and hands and arms and right thigh hurt a lot. Of course I had no idea how bad I looked, and the camera that recorded Prince Charles' visit didn't really show it either, because the worst part of the damage was on the right-hand side of my face, and the camera shot the visit mainly from my left.

I felt good as I cast around for something to talk about with the Prince when he arrived. I hit on the positive aspect of my experience in the wreckage of the train: my time with Craig. I'm sure I was over the top with good feeling (that survival adrenalin charge again) when I leant up and grabbed Prince Charles' arm and hand for a 'G'day, mate' the very moment he arrived and bent towards me.

The TV images on the Channel 4 news that evening could not give a sense of my feelings. There I am, on the television screen, lying nearly flat on my back in orange pyjamas, face puffy around the eyes, a big plaster on my head, and pretty passive. Compare this with the pictures in the 7 p.m. bulletin of another victim, Bruce Lait, a dancer, meeting the Queen at the Royal London Hospital. Bruce had similar damage to the face as me – shrapnel wounds, his all over the left side of the head, and hearing loss. However, he is sitting up, talking to the camera in one shot, to the Queen in another, whereas I look completely inactive, pinned to Bed 33, with my right arm waving about frenetically as I talk to the Prince. I began to feel pinned like this more and more later that day, as I realised that the only control

I had over my surroundings was the button that would gently ease my wonderful bed slowly up and down to help me avoid vomiting.

But I didn't think like that when Prince Charles was there, and, to his credit, he immediately warmed to my Aussie 'G'day, mate' approach. We swapped jokes for eight to ten minutes, and I told him of the carnage at Edgware Road, and about my guardian angel, Craig. I liked Prince Charles on that visit, one in a lifetime of thousands, for making me feel okay. I liked him not in the least because of who he is, but because of how he was with me that morning. It felt like an extension of the time that Craig and I had spent talking in the train like 'two guys on a park bench'.

The clip of Prince Charles and me on the Channel 4 news went out over the words, 'But on this Day 2 it has already meant for some facing the horror of yesterday', and the sombre tone was matched with a medium close-up of the Prince grimacing at something I was telling him. In fact, my own memory is of a very positive meeting, of laughing with him and feeling good. He left with another handshake and smile (the picture that got into newspapers worldwide), as he told me not to do anything dangerous and I said I wouldn't be presenting students at the Brunel University degree day the next Tuesday.

A matter of media ethics

And so Charles left, and the media frenzy set off by his visit began. The first journalist to get to me (there was a mob of them by now outside the hospital and in the foyer) was Chris Reason, an Australian from Channel 7 in Sydney. He told me he had arrived on the early flight that morning at Heathrow and, hearing about the royal visit, had come straight to the hospital. He had avoided the crush of journalists at the front desk and walked straight up to the ward to see me. This was about to cause a huge fuss, first with the hospital's public relations team, who were furious, and then in the Australian media more generally, as ABC TV's *Media Watch* devoted a major segment of its weekly programme and part of another to it. I don't know what Chris Reason said to the nurses at the ward desk – Aidan got pretty angry about it too – but I have to say that from the moment he came over to my bed he told me exactly who he was and what he had come for. My suspicion is that he was a bit less upfront before that, but he was sensitive and forthcoming with me, and I counted it as my second enjoyable chat of the day. Using a small digital camera, he also managed to get actual images of how bad I really looked to viewers in Australia.

As for me, it was in early meetings like this one with Chris and with Prince Charles that I began to think through and put together the otherwise discrete images of what happened the previous day. They were helping me reconstruct, as a continuous narrative, the sequence of events of that abnormal day.

Things began to go badly soon after that. The Channel 7 journalist had by now taken a few shots with his digital camera and I thought he said that his larger crew, and maybe his 'young female colleague with some flowers', would arrive later. Sure enough, I thought that had happened when a young woman appeared in the afternoon with a pot plant. But then my confusion began. Aidan introduced her as 'a friend of yours from Sydney'. I rolled over too quickly to my right to say hello, and got my first savage feeling of nausea and vertigo. My smile to her must have been rather strained, and my mind began losing its connections. I decided that this person was one of my Ph.D. students from Brunel (I still didn't have glasses and couldn't see features at all clearly through my puffy eyes anyway). She asked me the usual questions about what happened, as any visitor would. The feeling of sickness subsided, and so we talked on for quite a bit until she asked for my sons' telephone numbers in

Sydney (I must have mentioned them while talking about Craig on the train). This didn't seem like the agenda of a student, even though when I had asked her why she was here she talked about doing some writing. Anyway, finally the penny dropped with me and, in response to my probing, she told me she was a journalist for the *Daily Telegraph* in Sydney. Then she began to hassle me, taking what seemed like endless photographs, and I felt more and more nauseous.

That first, intense feeling of sickness I had in hospital marked out her visit as different from those of the other journalists, although this was not her fault at all. The other thing that differed is that she did not introduce herself as a journalist, either to Aidan at the desk or to me, and that was the crux of the major criticism of Australian journalists' ethics that swept St Mary's and soon enough the Australian media back home and the Australian High Commission in London.

Those moments with the Sydney *Sunday Telegraph* journalist on that afternoon marked the beginning of the biggest downer for me. After my first symptoms of vertigo when I lay in bed, I realised just how bad they could be when I tried walking in the ward. This happened after a specialist came to see me (I saw so many over the following eight days that I could never put a face to a function, either then or later). He was cheerful about my condition, having seen the previous day's test results, and he said I might even be out of hospital the next day. To be fair, he was simply mirroring my own earlier mood when, after Charles' visit, I had rung my head of school at Brunel to say that I would be back at work within ten days or a fortnight (when I was due to take over as acting head of school while he was on research leave). One of the things the specialist mentioned when we spoke was the possible threat of death from superbugs if I stayed long in hospital. This drove me to my feet and I took a few steps in the ward, hanging off someone's shoulder. The shock of being told I might die some other way was just too much at that moment. It was when I began to feel continuously the same vertigo sensation I had experienced briefly outside Edgware Road Station the previous day and had since forgotten all about.

My Fallujah fantasy

If you have not had vertigo – and I never had – it is hard to describe. It is as though everything falls away from you. Not that you are falling so much, as that everything else is falling, as everything substantial melts into thin air. The hospital ward floor became something that moved radically and had no intention whatsoever of supporting my feet. It felt like an extension of that destabilising and stretching yellow image I remembered of the explosion on the train. There was also an intense feeling of nausea. I decided I definitely wasn't ready to leave St Mary's.

And so began the horrible days of vomiting into my little crescent-shaped bowl, particularly every time I was moved in one of the hospital wheelchairs. The orderlies who pushed them did their job as best they could, but every time we reached a lift and the doors opened for other patients to come out, there was that little jiggle sideways that is the best friend of vertigo; and every time they wheeled me to the ward desk to take a call from Marian and family in Australia, I got the same dreadful feeling. The day my brother David visited me (Sunday, 10 July), I seemed to have been in a wheelchair the whole day, going for endless tests, so that for the full hour he was with me I vomited into that bowl – or rather into a whole stack of them sat in a tower on my bedside table. The bowl became my new talisman, replacing my lost bag, as the thing that went everywhere with me.

Vertigo and nausea made me very down for a couple of days. There were endless injections (sometimes painful, depending on which nurse it was who gave them), so that first my right arm got too bruised and swollen for any more aggression, and then increasingly my left one, when even the drip had to be removed. The pain in my head, kept at a distance by drugs, throbbed continually, and I grew more aware of my diminished hearing. When local friends and colleagues called me on the telephone, the journey to the phone and the sheer exhaustion of trying to hear what they were saying became so upsetting that I had to ask them to ration their calls.

There was also that damned urine bottle – an embarrassment when visitors came, but my constant, demanding companion either hidden in my sheets or sitting rampant on my side table, sometimes partially full. I had quickly devised a way of rolling on to my left side to use it beneath the sheets, but always worried about spillage if it got over-full.

It was at that time, during Friday afternoon and evening, that I began having my Fallujah fantasies. Iraq had been on my mind, of course, for a long time. I had gone with my family to the huge demonstration against the war on a sunny day in Sydney in February 2003. As a media academic I had been collecting material on the build-up to both the Kosovo and the Iraq wars in order to see which newspapers supported what, as between them they used quite a range of discourses for and against. Like everyone else, I had been shocked and outraged by the images coming out of Abu Ghraib, and I had gathered different newspaper accounts of that, too. Then came the attack on Fallujah, and I read about doctors (who collated the civilian victim lists that our side didn't seem to want to hear about) being 'targeted' (Naomi Klein's words that caused great offence to the US ambassador in London) and hospitals being destroyed in the first wave of attacks. So you could say I had a predisposition, intellectually and politically, to having my Fallujah fantasies.

However, I hadn't expected them in hospital. Even in my

confused, drug-sedated mind, I never thought that I was over there; I always knew exactly where I was. That was, though, part of the strength of the recurring fantasy. Physically I felt very bad, with a lot of pain and little control over my body and its functions. All I could do – and this was obvious to me after my abortive Thursday-afternoon walk in the ward – was press the bed button to raise and lower my upper body ever so slightly. With bad vertigo, an inch the wrong way, as you lift yourself or as you sit, can have dramatically awful effects. So, for example, when I first got to stand up and pee by myself the following Monday evening (hanging grimly on to a support bar), I thought all was well. But then I leaned forward and very slightly down to where the flush lever was on the lower half of the cistern, and my world collapsed into dreadful vertigo. After that I always went to a different toilet, where the cistern was at exactly the same height, but the flush lever was near the top, and I was okay. Everything is so precise and marginal with vertigo. I think it was the nature of my condition, and my inability (except with that wonderful bed button) to do anything about controlling it – plus the continuous pain – that led to my Fallujah fantasy. This was the closest I'd ever got to some of the pain people there must have experienced, trivial and remote though mine was in contrast. I also had the attention of what I was beginning to call security medicine, with nurses and specialist doctors around me all the time. But what, I thought, if they *weren't* there for me? And then the even worse thought, What if the damage to my head and arms and leg had happened in Abu Ghraib, and the soldiers came back to give me more and worse of the same? I shivered at these thoughts that evening in St Mary's, and when I looked up at the ceiling tiles in the ward as I waited for the lights to go off, the tiles moved and distorted themselves, like my carriage on the Circle Line had distorted itself. I definitely didn't feel as good as I had the night before.

THREE

9/10 July: First Images

For the first two days at St Mary's I didn't get to see any images of the terror attack. Janet had decided that the photographs of me emerging from Edgware Road Station might be too traumatic and bring it all back, and there were no newspapers circulating in the hospital. Nor did the Toynbee Ward have personal TV sets near most of the beds. I saw none of the many shots of myself and others at Edgware Road that were already circulating prominently in the world press.

But on Saturday, 9 July, and Sunday, 10 July, Janet and other friends began to relent and I saw for the first time what the newspapers were doing with the terror attack. My concussion meant that I couldn't read much – at most the odd paragraph beside a picture to begin with. I could, though, and did, look closely and lengthily at the photographs, like the ones of me and of Davinia Turrell emerging from Edgware Road. I began to perceive the way in which these images were already becoming iconic in representing the terrorist attacks. They were beginning to signify things that I could not control, and which by and large attributed to me motives and moods that I didn't necessarily share.

The photographs of both of us initially represented the terrible horror of the attack. As I have said, as part of a first stage of representing the disaster, the photographs of Davinia and myself were similar, but also seemed dramatically different. Mine initially appeared to me more an image of helplessness, confusion and displacement.

Yet not complete helplessness perhaps. As the days passed, the image was used in slightly different settings. On 18 July 'The London Plot' issue of *Newsweek* featured images from Edgware Road, including a double-page colour photograph of me (captioned, 'Bloodied. Unbowed'), across which were trailed Tony Blair's words, 'When they try to divide our people or weaken our resolve, we will not be divided, and our resolve will hold firm.' As part of a series of shots taken of me at Edgware Road, this image had me looking to my right and was cropped to include five ambulance and emergency service personnel, clearly representing the 'people' from the Blair quotation who will not be divided. My image, however 'bloodied', was now anchored by the word 'unbowed', since, together with all my resolute helpers, 'resolve will hold firm' against any terrorist attack.

I was a bit shocked by all of this, as Janet was worried I would be – especially those swollen, squinting eyes peering sideways at my emergency helpers. Later, though, I got a laugh as I noticed what it was my eyes were fixed on in some of the photos. I'm staring at my cabin bag, rescued for me by Craig on the train, but already taken from my hands and hanging on the back of one of the ambulance women. That, though, was for much later, when I was feeling a lot better and had already got that bag back. To begin with it was all serious stuff on that Saturday and Sunday, when I was on the downer of my roller-coaster.

A couple of things seemed immediately obvious to me. First, as we've seen, like all the media coverage of disaster and risk I had looked at over the years, the initial images were about victims and their helpers, showing that everything that could be right in the face of horrible aggression *was* right. The disaster plan was in place. Second, there was an immediate move into what I call 'Blitz resistance' mode.

The *Sun* newspaper's editorial 'True Brit Grit' on the Saturday was typical of what the media were saying at the time:

> Sixty years ago tomorrow, Britain finally beat Nazism. Men, women and children from every walk of life – not just the military – worked fearlessly and tirelessly to crush Hitler's tyranny. Gritty Londoners proved to be unbeatable. Many brave people sacrificed THEIR lives so that we may enjoy OURS in freedom today. Each was a hero in their own way. The nation stood firm and the nation won. Today Britain calls upon a new generation of heroes to fight an enemy every bit as sinister. Thursday's atrocities in London once more brought out the best of Britain. The *Sun* salutes the heroes of the ambulance service, the paramedics, the police, the fire brigade, doctors and nurses who gave of themselves to save life. But we also thank the army of ordinary folk who acted because it was the right thing to do . . . Brits are STILL made of the Right Stuff.

I didn't read this *Sun* editorial till later, but I didn't need to in order to get the spirit of what was around in the press. This had been an attack on London, so the Second World War analogy was invoked, visually and verbally, straight away. In the *Independent on Sunday* an image of a somewhat Churchillian-looking man gazed right out of the page, his head bandaged like mine, and another dressing beneath his chin. With blood trailing down his jacket and spotting his shirt, his tie still on, his (bloody) newspaper still held resolutely under his arm, and a bottle of mineral water and plastic cup held firmly in his hand, the image shows us that he is unbowed in the face of what the headline above his head trailed, 'Attack On London'. Next to him on the page there is a photograph of me, bandaged, bleeding and burnt, with my helpers, and next to that another victim from Edgware Road: a young, blonde woman, her face showing her tears, while she too is holding a bottle of Marks & Spencer's still water. These images take up half the page of the old-style *Independent* broadsheet, above Cole Moreton's piece, 'Minute by Minute the Horror Emerges'.

Moreton's big-print heading emphasises the immediate, the everyday, the pain and shock, and the courage of a London revisited by the Blitz. I was able to read his words: 'From the very first reports of trouble on the rush-hour trains, through the hours in which ordinary lives were touched by confusion, pain, sorrow and courage, Cole Moreton pieces together the definitive account of the day that terror returned without warning, to the streets of London.' There is another photo embedded in the middle of his piece, showing the motorway sign, 'Avoid London. Area Closed', and I could read enough of the article to see the heading '8.50 a.m. Edgware Road', followed by:

> War veterans say that if a bomb goes off and you do not hear the sound of it, then you are close enough to expect death. On his Circle Line train at Edgware Road Station, Chris Randall hears nothing. He just sees a flash of light and feels a burning sensation in his hand. 'I fell to the floor and covered my face with my hands'.

It was then I became especially aware that I hadn't heard the bomb either, and the comment about war veterans might tell me something about my proximity to the explosion. Until then I still thought the worst damage had been done in the first carriage, even though I knew by now this was a terror attack and not a train crash. Chris Randall's reported comments also cued me into remembering that urine-yellow flash of the explosion, which I had forgotten about as well.

For the first time, too, I was seeing in the newspapers the map of London which was to become a theme of the media's terror accounts, showing the sites where the bombs exploded – a 'flash' icon next to Aldgate, Edgware Road, King's Cross and Tavistock Square, which later was to be used graphically to show not just the ubiquity of terror in London, but to hypothesise the deadly 'cross of fire' that the terrorists were said to have intended. However, those maps sometimes also showed another cross, indeed a cluster of crosses, demonstrating the resistance to terror at the hospitals of St Mary's (near Edgware Road), University and Great Ormond Street (near King's Cross and Tavistock Square) and Royal London and Guy's and St Thomas' (near Liverpool Street and Aldgate).

The journalists had got the time wrong for the Edgware Road explosion in a lot of the early papers, with the bombers supposedly striking at 9.17 a.m. I knew it happened some time before my 9.15 a.m. train from Paddington, and I reckoned it was about 8.56 a.m. Nevertheless, the reporting was beginning to piece the narrative together for me, despite getting some details wrong. Much of it was concerned with showing how everything was being managed, as the *Guardian* on 8 July backed its 'Attack on London' map with a huge, whole-page colour photo of Davinia in her surgical burns mask with her resolute helper at Edgware Road.

Resolute, too, were the newspaper front pages of the next day. The *Sun* front page showed an inset of me above the can-opened bus at Tavistock Square with the headline: '53 Dead in London Terror Attacks. Our Spirit Will Never Be . . .' The *Daily Mirror* showed the shattered Circle Line carriage at Aldgate with the headline: '37 Dead, 700 Injured in London Suicide Terror. Blair Vows: Britain Will NOT Be Intimidated'.

In hospital Janet brought me the *Guardian* and the *Independent* mainly, and it was there that I began to string things together through pictures and the few short bits of articles that I could read. I saw my picture with Charles, a mutually smiling one with a firm handshake and the Prince's comment, 'What I can never get over is the resilience of the British people who have set us all a fantastic example of how to recover.' Saturday's *Guardian* also had an image which showed what the inside of my carriage had looked like two days before. It was a part of a piece describing the attack 'As it happens. Victims capture unfolding events on mobile phones.' Under hellish images of dark tunnels, blinding lights and shuffling lines of shadowy people, the article quoted two experts on the use of new technology in reporting. Executive editor at *Sky News* John Ryley says, 'The difference that mobile technology makes, it empowers . . . ordinary people to show what happened as it happens, not a minute later or an hour later. So you are seeing the drama, the story unfolding. The new technology takes you one step further.' Cynthia McVey, a psychologist, was also quoted: 'Some people can show remarkable presence of mind in life-threatening situations and doing that can afford them some control . . . The thing about these situations is that you have no control.'

So the take on new technology in this brief *Guardian* article was that it empowered people, and gave them a sense of control in the most extreme situations. Looking at the piece, I wondered whether I would have taken mobile shots if my phone hadn't been in my (then still lost) cabin bag. I'm not sure I was able to think much about this newspaper piece's idea of empowering technology at the time, but what I did get from the mobile-phone photographs in the paper was my first exact recollection of what it looked like as I sat on that burnt bench seat in carriage two, looking across the two American women to the lit-up Tube train that Craig Staniforth was about to jump in from. The *Guardian* photograph that particularly grabbed my attention looked just like what I had seen, with a figure in the dark foreground and lit-up Tube windows behind, where people were standing. The difference was that the figure in the foreground in the photo is active, his hand holding something across the mouth to keep out the choking smoke. The two bleeding American women, lying slumped on the seat and floor opposite me, didn't look like that. Still, the photograph offered me a precise visual recall of what happened two days before.

On that Saturday and Sunday, when I first saw images (and read a few words) about the terror attack, I was also trying to figure out how close I had been to the bomb. I gleaned some clues from these press reports. There was that comment about not hearing the explosion if you are very near to it. There was the mobile-phone image that reminded me of what it had all looked like seconds before Craig jumped in, and there was the reminder of the yellow-coloured flash by a fellow survivor in the same carriage. Until I saw these things, I was telling people (including police) that I had no memories of the explosion at all. In fact, I did have some memories, and I began to wonder whether there was more (and worse) that would suddenly be called up.

Images of some of the dead, and their stories, began to emerge at the weekend, and I found that very upsetting. I didn't at any point feel guilty that I was alive while they were dead, but I did feel the heart-rending stories of partners separated and families bereaved. I became obsessed with the fate of one young woman who the papers said had been killed at Edgware Road. They said she was coming from Reading to London, so I knew that she was unlikely to be on my train, which was going east to west. However, her being at Edgware Road seemed to be confirmed when a later story said she called her father in Bristol from Paddington on her mobile just minutes before the blast. I kept asking everyone I talked to about her. What train was she on? I especially plagued Ian, my police liaison officer who was based at St Mary's, with this. But no one could answer my question.

Why was I so obsessed with just one victim? I think perhaps for two reasons. One is that she came to personalise for me all the dead, and also all those people suffering as a result (like her vicar father in Bristol. Marian's father, too, had been a vicar in Bristol). The second reason is that by finding out about her I would know more of what happened in the tunnel near Edgware Road Station. And I wanted to know about that. The first newspaper reports not only got the time wrong, but the kind of bombing wrong and the number of trains damaged wrong. Some newspaper articles talked about at least two to three trains being wrecked by a single bomb that was possibly placed in an adjoining wall. I never gave much credence to that. Digging holes in a very public wall didn't seem to me what terrorists were likely to do, even if this theory would have explained how someone on a train coming in the other direction might have been killed.

I actually wondered at the time whether my concern to know what had happened to just one victim was voyeuristic. But even then I thought it was something else. The desire to know what went on around my train was another symptom of my sense of complete powerlessness as I lay in that hospital bed. Not only was I physically very vulnerable, I also didn't have a cognitive picture of what had happened to me; and with this dual feeling of disempowerment, my emotions were going into overdrive (as in my Fallujah fantasies). Which is not to say, of course, that those emotions were not real in fundamental ways. I was pleased to see in a newspaper photograph a few days later, for example, prominent placards in the Trafalgar Square rally calling for an end to terrorism in both London and Fallujah.

One photograph I saw on 9 July from the previous day's newspaper made me very angry. It was a shot of Prime Minister Tony Blair taken at Gleneagles just after he had been told about the terrorist attacks. He is standing alone, head bowed, and body stiff as though in genuine shock – or perhaps wired, like his US presidential friend, directly to God. My immediate thought was that it was a performance, a photo opportunity to gain empathy by a politician who, because of his illegal, media-spun military entry into Iraq, was deeply unpopular. For me, lying there that day, it was a posture well-practised, an attitude thought about and rehearsed long before.

If you think that was the cynical response from a much-weakened and highly emotional observer, then consider this: we had been told many times by police chiefs that a terrorist attack was inevitable in London – not if, but when. Would you, then, in Blair's position, not be prepared by thinking through every aspect of your response to a terror attack when it happened? And then think, additionally, about how very much more media-focused and obsessed Blair is than you are. Of course he would be ready, with his every physical and emotional and lin-guistic gesture rehearsed; which is, of course, perfectly reasonable, except for three things.

One, he is among the very few people left in the UK, as the leading Conservative politician Kenneth Clarke (and so many others) has observed, who seem to believe that the war in Iraq did not, at the very least, provide excellent recruitment propa-ganda and, indeed, practical experience for terrorists. Second, there was the decision of Blair's people to lower the level of anti-terrorism security for Londoners after the May general election, even while providing massive security for him at the G8 summit at Gleneagles. I imagined that large numbers of police and security forces were looking to Scotland that day, not the London transport system. And yet terrorists linked to the ideas of al-Qaeda have always acted with symbolic precision. They are not, *pace* the US President (Bush) and two premiers (Blair and Howard), 'mindless'. Indeed, they tend to act with clear, overt, meaningful intent; like, for example, making a major attack on the economy, and thus the psychology, of London by disrupting some of its major communication chains, and choosing, symbolically, the time when world leaders were meeting in Britain. So, given all our knowledge of the way terrorists operate, why was there lower security in London on 7 July?

Third, even worse from my point of view, my own image was beginning to be used in the media to bolster Blair's 'statesman-like' bravado, as in the *Newsweek* photograph of me across which were trailed his words, 'When they try to divide our people or weaken our resolve, we will not be divided, and our resolve will hold firm.' Well, sorry, Tony Blair, I thought, but it was you, over the Iraq war, who divided the British people more controversially than most prime ministers in our history. It was you who weakened the resolve of large swathes of the Labour Party membership by getting into bed with neo-liberalism (and Rupert Murdoch), using your mantra about Old Labour being lost in the past of ideology. It was you who jumped aboard the wagon train of the most ideologically committed and imperialistically focused US political party in decades.

The weekend of 9 and 10 July I was at my lowest ebb: vomiting throughout my brother David's hour-long visit; worrying that my niece Tracey's children Camilla and Daryl might be scared off by my horrible face when the family came to visit on Sunday (they weren't scared, and left lovely drawings of me instead); and being helped laboriously across the ward to the toilet by my Viennese friend Gerhard, who took a set of digital shots of me looking very bad indeed. The use of my suffering to bolster the Blair ideology of a new resolve around 'democracy' did not go down well with me – and it underpinned most newspaper accounts as well as the parliamentary consensus around Blair's statesmanship in the week following the attacks. Symptomatic was the London *Evening Standard*'s page on the 'Injured Survivors' on 8 July. The Duchess of Cornwall's comment, 'It makes me proud to be British', anchors the three photographs on the page, two of which happen to be of me. The biggest photo is that smiling handclasp between me and Prince Charles, then there are two smaller photos: of the Duchess meeting 'one of the 24 bomb victims taken to St Mary's' (who is also smiling cheerfully); and of me being cared for by paramedics at Edgware Road. Collected together the photographs tell a tale, of moving swiftly from a narrative absence (the bombed picture of me) to one of completion (the two smiling, well-cared-for, royalty-visited victims at St Mary's); and it is my 'smiling resilience' which helps makes us all 'proud to be British'.

I felt a minor irony in the fact that two of the three images are of an Australian who had his British passport removed in 1994. But that aside, I was beginning to feel co-opted for a 'Proud to be British' campaign that overlaid the long history (since before the Iraq war) of incompetence – like all those so-called weapons of mass destruction which took us to war to do some things that do not make a lot of Britons proud. So, yes, I did get quite angry when I saw the image of PM Blair.

Still, there were lots of uplifting things happening, too. Colleagues began to visit, including my head of school, who was helpful about a potentially lengthy spell for me off work, and Liz, our senior research administrator, with flowers and positive news about her own daughter, who had been close to two of the blasts. Students came to see me, like Stephen, my Ph.D. candidate who was close to submitting after a long and tortuous experience at three different British universities. My niece Tracey and her husband Stuart brought Daryl and Camilla. Anne, a media student of mine from twenty years previously, and now a leading Australian journalist visiting Europe with the New South Wales Premier, dropped by completely unexpectedly; as did John, a former colleague from Charles Sturt University in Australia, having walked all the way to Paddington from Russell Square Station, where, on 7 July, he had seen walking wounded pouring out from that attack. Janet was a constant visitor, quietly absorbing and tempering my ludicrous belief that I would be out of hospital on Monday, and talking with the hospital's occupational therapy staff about making her flat more vertigo-friendly for when I did get out.

And emails were pouring in. The journey to read them on the ward's intranet facility was itself nausea-inducing, because I always went in the wheelchair and felt vertigo just sitting at the screen. But the messages made up for it: the offer of books to read from Graham, who had originally met my wife Marian and me at Sydney Airport when we first arrived from the UK in 1973 and whom I had lost touch with twenty years before; and also from Dana, an American film academic whom I had never met. There were emails from terribly shocked and very close friends, and emails from Australians I had never met both in Britain and at home.

An Australian in London whom I didn't know sent me a packet of Tim Tams to 'cheer me up and make me think of home'. Another left a handwritten note at the hospital desk which, in its anonymity, was as cheering as any I got:

> *Dear john tulloch*
> *Hi john, you don't know me and I don't know you but I read about*
> *your circumstances in the TNT magazine this morning and couldn't*
> *help but try and cheer you up.*
> *Best wishes with your recovery.*
> *Fellow Aussie,*
> *Carley.*

And Ian, my police liaison – who was very important to me in these days as the only constant professional reference point among an almost daily-changing scenario of doctors and nurses – brought me a whole basket of Australian goodies donated by the Australia Shop. My family in Australia were able to get through the hospital embargo on phone calls (put on in response to the media frenzy after Prince Charles' visit), and these calls were enlivened by the close interest taken in them by the bizarre patient in the ward who often led the nurses a merry dance (especially when he would emerge either totally naked or in a duffel coat from his separate room, to be chased through the corridors and back to bed by the long-suffering hospital staff).

So even on these, my two lowest days, there was a lot going on that was positive, quirky and funny. And – as hospital patients seem to do in old war movies – I was beginning to take to one after another of the nurses! Every one of them had a particular quality of close empathy and professionalism that I needed very badly right then.

FOUR

7 July to 21 July:
Finding the Bad Guys

My time at St Mary's Hospital lasted from 7 July to 15 July, and the last four days, from Monday to Thursday, were marked for me by two turbulent things: my increasing difficulties with vertigo, and the country's angst-ridden recognition that the bombers who attacked us were 'home-grown'. Both were very uncomfortable struggles with identity.

On my feet at home

The nausea and vomiting associated with vertigo were constant and unpleasant. Nurses were trying to control the sickness with tablets, which meant a minor trauma for me each morning of, 'Will the pill come before the breakfast trolley?' Usually it did. But if it didn't, I would bring up my breakfast immediately. And even if it did, I still brought up my breakfast often enough.

My biggest hospital enemy was still the wheelchair, since I nearly always vomited after being wheeled to some medical check or other. A moment of disastrous hubris in this regard came on Monday, 11 July, during my first visit to the audiology lab at St Mary's. After my previous day's vomiting – embarrassingly in front of my brother for the full hour of his visit – I resisted the suggestion that I be wheeled to the audiology lab. Nurses told me it was quite a long way, down the lift and in another building, but I persevered, and was assigned someone to help me walk there.

The experience was awful. First, there was the lift; a new thing for me post-vertigo, and I waited for it, standing uncertainly with my carer, in trepidation. Once in the lift, the effect of the downwards motion on me was not as bad as I had feared, but when the doors opened at the ground level I was totally confused: the speed of action of the British public nearly knocked me over. In the hospital lobby, people, young and old, seemed to be flying by the open lift doors in their carefree summer clothes, and I realised straight away what a long journey of recovery I had in front of me.

The audiology lab wasn't just in another building, it was across a small hospital road, and I was appalled by my first sight of moving vehicles since the attacks. My carer helped me across carefully, but next I was faced with a long, downward-sloping corridor in the dingy audiology building itself. My feet slipped on the lino, and my damaged right hand grasped the single rail desperately as we stumbled down for what seemed like half an athletics lap. I eventually made it to the lab and had the test, but by then I had lost my resolve, and the carer was asked to bring me back to bed in my wheelchair.

Walking unaccompanied in the ward, usually to the toilet, was another desperate experience. It was great to be on my feet. Nonetheless, my first walk on Monday evening (and for the rest of that week in hospital) was a slow shuffle, with my eyes fixed ahead and down, and my arms stretched out to the front for balance, as I moved between beds, and between patients whom I could hardly hear and certainly couldn't see. Some of them may have wanted to talk, but I felt like a robot going by. I just could not look sideways. I was always afraid of falling, especially at night. In the toilet itself once I had to stand in the puddle left by another night-time traveller who had missed the target, because I didn't have the balance and flexibility to stand anywhere else. I told myself this was still better than staying in bed and wrestling with the urine bottle, and it was. It became a matter of self-image and independence and of somehow moving forward.

It was during one of those early night-time visits to the loo that I caught the first glimpse of my damaged face. As I hung on grimly with one hand to the wall bar next to the toilet bowl, and leant across to the basin to wash my other hand, I had two quick looks at my face in the mirror, and it wasn't cool at all, but surprisingly upsetting.

This marked the start of a growing recognition that my optimism in the first two days after the bombings was wide of the mark. There was an awful lot to do (though I hadn't any idea quite how much), and even my departure from the hospital on Thursday, 15 July, was physically fraught. It was decided that I should leave by a back entrance, in case any of the media were still at the front. So Erin, my young Australian occupational therapist, began to push me in a wheelchair across an uneven tarmac surface which seemed more like that of the moon. The tar had melted in those hot July days and was so pockmarked and rocky that I couldn't manage it without vomiting. We had to walk the last thirty metres, and then I had to be strapped flat on a stretcher in the ambulance because I couldn't sit up in the seats without vertigo.

It wasn't an auspicious way to leave hospital, but on the other hand it was a reality check. I was no longer the survivor of 7 July, but a struggler on a slow yet upward path, and I was being given clear and positive markers towards my new identity.

Erin had been to Janet's flat before to establish problem

points in relation to my vertigo: the four flights of stairs up to the flat; and the height of the toilet seat, armchair and bed. She chose the most suitable armchair and made it and the toilet seat higher with simple, solid frames. This was absolutely crucial to me in managing my vertigo. I would walk to my raised chair, turn my back to it very slowly and use those same hands that had nearly pushed me up from my train seat and into the bomb just one week earlier, to feel carefully for the seat level and stop myself sitting down too fast. Vertigo sufferers don't like quick movements, sideways, up or down. In the bathroom, a board had been fixed securely across the bath, and each morning, very early, a carer would visit to help me undress, lift one leg then the other into the bath, help me sit on the board and then wash my head, legs and body. It was necessary to avoid getting water in my damaged ears, so in my first days out of hospital Erin had to be there as well, to show the succession of different carers how to wash my hair, while I had to learn how to prepare my water-proof cotton-wool earplugs. Modesty was not something to bother about, as a variety of carers, one, two, sometimes three at a time, looked after my body.

It was a wonderful support service: from Erin, my occupa-tional therapist, Maggie, my physiotherapist, and something like a dozen different ladies who helped me bathe. I used to chat with those carers, mostly student nurses, but one a young com-puter student at Brunel University. Within that fantastic outpatient service, I was able to find new friends and a renewed identity. As Maggie emphasised, it had to be one built using the kind of patience that I had never had, setting small targets reg-ularly and not being upset if a particular target was not achieved. I remember very clearly the first time I was able to walk across Janet's sitting room from my chair to the window, quite unconsciously shifting her grandson's little yellow plastic chair out of my way with one leg as I went. It was only after I had done it that I realised I had stood momentarily on one leg to move the chair with the other. It was a euphoric feeling. Equally, I remember vividly the day soon after, when I was standing wet and naked next to the bath with my carer, and told her I thought I could dry my own leg by putting it up on the bath, again standing on one leg. It was through those two achievements that I regained my confidence at home – in Janet's flat at least (I was a long way from getting to my own flat in Cardiff, let alone being able to live there). The result was that I could demarcate stages of achievement and progress and could set new challenges: for example, I would not attempt to enter the outside world until I had gained confidence in the inside world of Janet's flat; and I would not consider going back again on London's buses and Tubes until I had gained much more confidence on my feet in the outside world.

In their own sphere, I quickly became as impressed with my professional carers, especially Erin and Maggie, as I had been with Craig on the wrecked train. They shared the qualities of quiet professionalism, precision, pragmatism and objective empathy, all of which I hadn't experienced, perhaps had not ever needed to experience, before. For instance, on my first very nervous and hesitant journey outside with Maggie – a walk of no more than twenty metres to sit in a small park in front of Janet's flat – we discussed my anxiety about people's move- ment, which I had first been aware of as I exited the lift at St Mary's. Maggie noticed a nearby bus stop on the very busy Hampstead Road just outside the park, and said I should set myself the small target of one day sitting on the bench in that bus shelter. There I would be protected on three sides and seated – no need to worry about my balance or being knocked over – and would be able to encounter the concentrated groups of people getting off and on the bus. Later, when I had done this and announced to Maggie that my next target should be to walk, accompanied, in the busy Camden High Street, she told me that I would need to be able 'to duck and weave'. She took an orange from Janet's fruit bowl and started throwing it to me, at my chest, to my sides and up or down, all high-risk areas for generating vertigo. She was watching my reaction to see whether I snatched at it with that narrow-eyed, sideways glance I show towards my bag in the Edgware Road photographs, or whether I moved my body to the orange by ducking and weaving. It didn't matter whether I caught it, because this wasn't a test of reaction time. She wanted to see whether I could duck and weave, and after twenty minutes of that she said I was ready for Camden High Street.

These small targets – the little yellow chair; the foot up on the bath; the bus stop; ducking and weaving in Camden High Street; then later my first taxi ride in company; my first train ride in company; my first Tube trip in company; and finally doing all these things on my own, including standing up in the shower and washing my own hair without getting water in my ears – were my pathway to progress. As I reconstructed my own sense of identity, I began to value things about my body that I had never even noticed before. And it was achieved by way of the care and empathy of working people that I had never before experienced. Some of these things took months to achieve, and some still have not been achieved, but the path to mastering vertigo is under my control.

My other problems of concussion and especially hearing have been harder to deal with. In my first weekend at Janet's flat after leaving hospital I spent much of my time in bed watching the Open Golf Championship on TV from St Andrews. I couldn't handle fast movement or quick editing on the screen, so the golf was perfect, with its long, slow preparation shots. I could watch the ball in the air without having to look up, and all the dramatic putting was covered by a static camera and patient expectation. Hearing the sound, though, was another matter. The TV was on so loud – and still I couldn't hear it well – that Janet worried about complaints from the neighbours.

It was during that weekend that I'd first met Maggie, who sat with Erin around my bed, speaking softly and clearly, giving me my first tips to help with vertigo. As I was watching the golf, the police detective constable also came. (He had encountered his own tragedy since I last saw him: his colleague had been killed.) He patiently took my report. I could remember a bit more than when I had seen him ten days earlier. He asked me whether I had seen the bomber, since by this stage we knew it had been a suicide bomber. I mentioned that I now had this memory of two men, one of whom looked Pakistani while the other was much darker, sitting on the bench seat opposite and looking across at me. I emphasised that although this wasn't a fantasy, that I had seen these two men some time on the Tube train that week, I could not say for certain whether it was on that particular journey. When he read back to me the verbatim notes he had taken, he missed out that 'not say for certain' bit, and I insisted that he include it, because I could see the implications. Was there a fifth man involved, with two on my train? I wasn't confident enough in my memory to start that kind of goose hunt.

Now though, looking back, I am beginning to think it must have been on that train that I saw the two men, because all the other Tube trains I had caught that week – the Metropolitan Line trains to Uxbridge and back to Euston Square – don't have bench seats.

Meanwhile, even as I watched the golf and talked with the detective constable, the media were busy with their own ways of connecting my and other victims' images with those of the suicide bombers.

Home-grown bad guys – finding the bombers

At exactly the same time that I was struggling to my feet in the hospital and then beginning to gain confidence in my new surroundings at Janet's flat, the British public began to lose confidence in the notion that bad guys are always other, always from outside our local space.

By Wednesday, 13 July, the media were well into a 'punish the guilty' phase, and it was now they revealed that the terrorists were not only suicide bombers (much harder to control and catch) but also were home-grown. On that day I took part in a bedside press conference that the hospital public relations department arranged for me with journalists from British and Australian newspapers and television. In the following day's *Daily Mail* I was given a double-page spread, with two large pictures. One, the familiar Edgware Road photo of me, was captioned, 'Victim of terror ... whose blood-stained face became a symbol of survival', and the other, a recent hospital shot in my (now green) pyjamas, was labelled, 'Smiling through his injuries'.

In this media representation of the positive, the headline was, 'Covered in Blood, But I Was ALIVE'; and the opening line was, 'With his head covered in bandages and blood, his picture became one of the defining images of the terror attacks'. Well, I certainly did feel alive and was very positive about that, as I told them, but arguably the newspaper also needed these positives, because over the page you will find something very negative indeed in Melanie Phillips' critique of British Muslims and the British elite:

> In this devastating personal critique, Melanie Phillips argues that many British Muslims are in denial over the extremists in their midst. Meanwhile our elite is more concerned about NOT upsetting Muslim feelings than in extirpating the evil of suicide bombers. This lunacy, she says, must stop.

Near to Phillips' 'devastating critique' are the *Daily Mail*'s early biographies of the recently revealed suicide bombers.

Under the heading, 'Cricketer Whose Family Owns a Fish and Chip Shop', the newspaper begins its own deconstruction of the chaos at the heart of British symbols:

> Behind his easy smile and gentle manner, Shehzad Tanweer, 22, had become increasingly consumed by religious fervour culminating in a two-week trip to an Islamic camp in Pakistan at the beginning of this year . . . Tanweer, who sometimes helped out in his father's fish and chip shop, was cautioned by police last year for disorderly conduct. Otherwise he has all the qualities Muslim extremists would look for in a 'cleanskin' recruit – he was young, impressionable and idealistic.

This is the geography and the demonology of Britain's right-wing press: the symbols of the domestic base (cricket, fish and chip shop) shown to be penetrated and defiled by a naive and impressionable young man who has been got at in that most dangerous of fanatical sites, 'an Islamic study camp in Pakistan'. Get rid of that – or at least the connection with impressionable boys who work in our fish and chip shops – and you will get rid of terrorism, implies the *Mail*.

Of course, there were differences between newspapers in their degree of backing-Britain bravado, as I was able to observe in close-up that week. The *Sun*, one of Rupert Murdoch's vast international fleet of newspapers that unanimously supported the Iraq war, has been a particularly strident member of his team, inflecting its proud-to-be-British stance with its regular line on 'backing our boys' (that is, our military boys) and lambasting as 'British traitors' anyone who opposes the war. And so it was that the *Sun* came (with the approval of the Ministry of Defence) to see me in hospital on Wednesday, 13 July, with one of 'our boys' whom, I would certainly agree, the newspaper did have a right to be proud of: Wing Commander Craig Staniforth, who, as the paper accurately reported, had 'leaped from another train, over live rails, into the bombed carriage'.

The St Mary's Hospital press office, already appalled at and suspicious of certain parts of the media after Prince Charles' visit, had earlier approached me to set up a meeting with Craig on my last full day in hospital, but had cautioned me that he would be bringing newspaper journalists with him. They said it would be the *Sun*, and that I had a right to veto it if I wanted to. My response was that I owed Craig so much, if he wanted the *Sun*, so be it. I was intrigued as to his choice of newspaper companion. When I asked him later about this, Craig said that the Ministry of Defence made these decisions. I presume it had reason to know that the *Sun* could be depended upon. From Craig's point of view, the other services – police, emergency, etc. – had already had a good run in the newspaper, and he wanted his outfit to be visible there too. This is why he brought his RAF uniform with him for the photograph. Craig later told the *Observer* about the experience of meeting me again:

> The first Craig knows about it is when Australian news channels start to call him. John has given a radio interview mentioning Craig; would he now like to come and meet John in hospital? Yes, he was desperate to learn what had become of the man he'd left at M&S. But there would be cameras there. Craig worried that he might cry. Or would it be a stiff-upper-lip handshake? He arrives at the ward, nervous, hears a voice he recognises behind the hospital curtains. John is with his physiotherapist, and then he spots him. 'Oh hi, Craig. Just a second. Let me deal with this.' Craig relaxes instantly. This is not going to be too sad, too emotional. This is going to be two men meeting who are pleased to see each other again.

It was great to see Craig again, and there is a nice photo in the *Sun* with him in his Air Force uniform and me in my green pyjamas still looking a bit the worse for wear facially. And there's yet another firm handshake. However, the photo and article about us didn't in fact quite take up the whole page of the paper the next day. Beside it was what 'The *Sun* says', which was: 'Show them we are not afraid':

> At noon today we show the world why we are stronger than al-Qaeda and its pathetic disciples. For two minutes Britain will stand in silent defiance. If you can, leave your home or workplace. Go out in the street. Be visible – Britons of all races and religions publicly demonstrating that terror will always fail. Do it – especially if you are a Muslim.

That was indeed a day of mass demonstrations in the street (although the photograph of Tony Blair outside appeared to show him skulking bravely in the 10 Downing Street back garden, surrounded by police, while Ken Livingstone and other public figures spoke in open spaces). It was from the photos of these mass demonstrations that I spotted the placards about state terrorism in Fallujah. But the *Sun* believed the answer to terrorism was for 'the Muslim community' to end 'the sick teachings of rogue preachers', 'silence them, drive them out of the community centres and mosques' so that they cannot 'infect young minds'. There is only so much, the paper says, that the police and MI5 can do. So it is up to British Muslims to 'be alive to the spread of dangerous extremism – spot it and root it out' – just as, with the *Sun*'s wholehearted approval, we were 'rooting out' extremism in Iraq.

Elsewhere, in its comment next to the photo of Craig and me, the paper says that there is something else that police and security forces can do:

> Our security forces must be given further powers to protect us. Let them eavesdrop on phone calls and emails. Let them

close down British websites spreading al-Qaeda propaganda and force Europe's internet service providers to make foreign ones inaccessible. Do whatever it takes. And do it now. Ignore the whining civil liberties brigade. *We can worry about the erosion of minor personal freedoms once Britain has been made safe to enjoy them.*

The headline next to this *Sun* editorial, at the top of the article on Craig and myself, was, 'John: I'll Buy Bomb "Angel" a Large Beer'. So, on that one page we have clearly established for us the *Sun*'s mythology of devils (of 'perverted, insane faith') and angels ('the RAF officer'). Ironically the newspaper had unintentionally promoted a public handshake of one of its heroes with what it would regard as a member of the 'whining civil liberties brigade'.

Fortunately, in my view at least, that brigade does still have a voice in the British media, as I observed in the period after this article appeared and before the second terrorist attack on 21 July. By then I had already read Robert Fisk's piece 'The Reality of this Barbaric Bombing' in the *Independent*:

'If you bomb our cities', Osama bin Laden said in one of his recent video tapes, 'we will bomb yours' . . . It was crystal clear Britain would be a target ever since Tony Blair decided to join George Bush's 'war on terror' and his invasion of Iraq. We had, as they say, been warned. The G8 summit was obviously chosen, well in advance, as Attack Day . . . It is easy for Tony Blair to call yesterday's bombings 'barbaric' – of course they were – but what about the civilian deaths of the Anglo-American invasion of Iraq in 2003, the children torn apart by cluster bombs, the countless innocent Iraqis gunned down at American military checkpoints? When they die, it is 'collateral damage'; when 'we' die, it is 'barbaric terrorism'.

This theme was taken up by a piece I also read by Robin Cook in the *Guardian* on 15 July, 'Our Troops are Part of the Problem':

> [T]here is no escaping the hard truth that the chaos in [Iraq] is a direct result of the decision to invade it, taken in defiance of the intelligence warning that it would heighten the terrorist threat . . . Statistics compiled by the Iraqi health ministry confirm that twice as many civilians have been killed by US military action than by terrorist bombs.

Front-page data in the *Independent* on 20 July took this further via new figures compiled by the Iraq Body Count and Oxford Research Group. I now read that 'Allied forces were the sole killers of 9,270 of the victims . . . anti-occupation forces were the sole killers of 2,353'. At the same time, there were reports in the media about the uses and abuses of intelligence by Tony Blair. On 19 July, the *Guardian* security affairs editor, Richard Norton-Taylor, wrote about both Whitehall intelligence committees' warnings in February 2003 and those of certain think tanks in July 2005 of the link between an invasion of Iraq and increasing terrorism. Articles like these did the public a service by drawing attention to decisions and documents which the public should have known about long before. Thus Norton-Taylor writes:

> The security and intelligence agencies, along with most among the senior ranks of Whitehall, opposed the invasion of Iraq on the grounds that it could not be justified . . . 'Intelligence and facts were being fixed around the policy', Sir Richard Dearlove, then head of MI6, told a meeting chaired by Blair on July 23 2002, the minutes of which were leaked to the *Sunday Times* . . . Another secret Whitehall memo, also

leaked, was drawn up for ministers on July 21 2002, eight
months before the invasion. It urged them to prepare the
'conditions', not for the reconstruction of post-Saddam Iraq
or to prevent an insurgency, but to con the British people.
The memo spoke of the need to 'create the conditions necessary to justify military action . . . Time will be required to
prepare public opinion in the UK that it is necessary to take
military action against Saddam Hussain'.

A *Guardian* editorial that I read on 20 July also drew attention
to both the Chatham House think tank and Whitehall's Joint
Terrorism Analysis Centre having recently pointed to Iraq 'as
motivation and a focus of a range of terrorist-related activity in
the UK'. It added that it is 'reasonable to assume that British
Muslims might have been more cooperative in helping the
authorities monitor extremism had it not been for Fallujah, Abu
Ghraib and Guantanamo Bay'. Similarly, in the *Evening Standard*
of 19 July, I read Ken Livingstone saying that the Iraq war may
well have inspired the bombers:

> We created these people. We built them up. We funded them.
> This has been a terrible legacy. This will have some impact
> on how these young men's minds were formed. This particu-
> lar strand of extremism was funded by the West in
> Afghanistan. Osama bin Laden was just another businessman
> until he was recruited by the CIA.

In the same paper on 15 July I saw a piece from a young
Muslim's point of view by Imran Khan, who had interviewed
Faisal, a twenty-six-year-old second-generation immigrant and
computer graduate from a south London university, who spoke
of the oppressive social, economic, educational, housing and
identity issues behind what the media were calling home-grown
terrorism:

Of all Britain's immigrant communities, Pakistanis feel they have been the most misunderstood. They have none of the glamour of Indian culture – Bollywood, 'Asian babes', a vibrant music scene. They have none of the perceived style or sounds of the African-Caribbean community . . . 'You ask any Muslim – liberal, moderate, extreme or orthodox – they will tell you that Islam makes them who they are. Islam gives you a powerful identity . . . Muslims see the murder of Palestinians, violence in Chechnya, Iraq, etc., and they feel that pain and that pain becomes anger.'

Imran had seen Faisal's graphic DVDs of atrocities committed against and by Muslims, and was shocked by what he saw:

Things have changed for Muslims in the four years I have known Faisal. He has become increasingly vocal in his opposition and hatred of the West . . . 'Remember, the guys behind this [7 July bombing] were not poor, or crazy loners. They had credit cards and played cricket but they did not feel part of the society. The only way to stop them would be to help bring dignity back to the way you treat Islam in Britain. Stop the war in Iraq, in Palestine, Kashmir, Chechnya. Stop funding corrupt Arab governments who stifle Islam and political debate, stop appointing community representatives who dismiss young Muslims, repeal the anti-terror laws, stop arresting hundreds of young Muslims without reason and understand that for a Muslim, Britain is his home but Islam is his heart.'

A few days later, I noticed that a *Guardian* editorial was citing an ICM poll indicating that there are 'tens of thousands' of Faisals in Britain. 'The poll found that 5% of all British Muslims – and 7% of Muslims under the age of 35 – think that further attacks by British suicide bombers would be "justified" . . . If you were unfortunate enough to die in such a bombing, in

other words, tens of thousands of your fellow citizens would justify your death to themselves.'

Then I read Jonathan Freedland on 20 July in the *Guardian*
berating on the one hand Tony Blair, Jack Straw and 'a good
chunk of the media' for claiming that the Iraq war and the 7/7
bombings were not related, and on the other hand noting a
Guardian/ICM poll of the previous day suggesting that two
thirds of the British population think there is an over-simple
causal link between the Iraq war and terrorism. Freedland
pointed to evidence of four kinds against Blair's position. First,
Britain had not been a jihadist target before 9/11. Second, it
was not only the anti-war movement but British intelligence
itself which had predicted that the threat from al-Qaeda would
be increased by the invasion. And third:

> is the evidence of our own eyes. Iraq has become what
> Afghanistan was before 2001, one huge university campus of
> terror. Analysts used to need a microscope to find links
> between Iraq and international terror . . . Now the place is
> positively crawling with active jihadists planting bombs,
> beheading hostages and plotting 57 varieties of mayhem in
> Europe and the West.

Fourth, and most important, he notes the then-current BBC
series by Peter Taylor, *The New Al-Qaeda*, in which Taylor had
spent a year interviewing Muslims in Spain, Morocco, the US,
Pakistan and the UK. According to Taylor, 'the one word' that
has served internationally to anger and radicalise a generation
of young Muslims 'is Iraq. There is no question that Iraq is the
prime motivating factor'. But Freedland also criticises the simple
causal link postulated by many anti-war supporters:

> Al-Qaida has a programme that predates and goes beyond
> Iraq. It seeks to end all western presence in those lands it

deems Islamic. That's why it has, over the years, targeted France and Germany, as well as the US and the UK. When Tony Blair asks 'What was September 11 the reprisal for?' he should know the answer. It was for eight decades of US-led, western meddling in territory that al-Qaida believes should be Muslim alone . . . In the [mid-1990s] Chechnya, Kosovo and Israel-Palestine all came into play – again predating Iraq . . . Iraq has played a key part – of course it has – in angering large numbers of young Muslims, pulling them towards an extremist message once confined to the lunatic fringe. But that message is not only about Iraq, Afghanistan or even the Israeli occupation of the West Bank and Gaza – and we delude ourselves if we think it is.

Just one day after Freedland's *Guardian* article came the further terrorist action of 21 July on London Underground trains and buses. And on 23 July Mark Lawson wrote a piece in the *Guardian*, 'On the Tube Dread Felt Deeper', that paralleled my own mood:

On July 8, it was possible for survivors to think that we had missed the city's big bad luck. On July 22, the sense was not of sombre gratitude for escape but grim acceptance of the possible beginning of a pattern. According to check lists on the internet, based on Israeli experience, one way of spotting a suicide bomber on public transport is to look out for passengers who seem sweaty or anxious or who are mouthing silent prayers . . . On the Central Line train eastward to Oxford Street, the majority of passengers were, by the internet visible anxiety test, potential suicide bombers. Except that they knew they were not, and so their eyes kept swivelling sideways in suspicion of others, like a politician's bodyguard. The toughest adjustment for Londoners is the introduction to a world in which the glimpse of a rucksack is like seeing a gun in the street.

Mark Lawson's description of Londoners' 'grim acceptance of the possible beginning of a pattern' after the abortive 21/7 attacks, and Tim Dowling's comment in the *Guardian*'s *G2* section on 26 July, 'I can pretty well pinpoint the moment when my own spirit of defiance started to fade', matched my own experience, as I, too, began to fear people with backpacks. It may seem strange to say, but 21/7 left me feeling far more afraid than the terrible 7/7 attacks that seriously injured me. Like others, I also thought of it as a pattern taking shape. Lying in my bed at Janet's flat, I listened to the ominous sound of police helicopters on 21 July (Warren Street Station, where one of the failed attacks took place, was only a stone's throw away) and remembered that my sons were due to fly into London from Australia that weekend to help me recuperate. I was now more fearful for them than for myself.

I believe this feeling was also because of the massive alienation the Blair government's foreign policy has caused not just in the Muslim communities, but across different British non-Muslim communities as well. Iraq connotes so many different, but equally powerful things to Britain's disaffected people. It connotes the presidential-style politics of a Prime Minister who fundamentally does not believe in democracy at all (witness Rupert Murdoch's later, mischievous revelation of Blair's fury at the 'anti-American' role of the BBC in covering the racist outrage that was the US government's response to the New Orleans floods). It means to many people a widespread revulsion at the British-backed US activities at Abu Ghraib, Fallujah and Guantánamo Bay. To yet others, represented in the media during these July weeks by Ken Livingstone, Iraq signifies many years of exploitation by the West of the economic resources in Muslim countries. It represents, also, a recognition of the realpolitik of cynical Western governments and the support by their intelligence agencies for Osama bin Laden and Saddam Hussein (and indeed the supply to the latter of 'weapons of mass destruction').

However, while the *Daily Mail* journalists would have been reading many of the same newspaper pieces that I had in those days between 15 and 21 July, they were certainly not taking much note of them, even less finding it necessary to debate the issues raised. Rather, with headlines about the abortive suicide bombers like, on 26 July, 'Terrorists on the Run had Shared Council Flat for Years'; 'The Bombers on Benefits'; and on the following day, 'Gratitude! These Families Came Here Seeking Asylum and Were Given Homes, Schooling and All the Benefits of British Life. How Do They Repay Us? By Trying to Blow Us Up'. The paper also printed photos of very black, 'Eritrea-born' and 'Somalian' men to continue promoting the conservative immigration line it had peddled for years.

Between 8 July and 21 July, the *Daily Mail* had been tracing its own inflection around the 'Blitz' image of the victims. As a Conservative as well as conservative newspaper, which was both hostile to the Blair government and to the Iraq war, the *Mail* twisted the knife into New Labour as much as it could, while remaining resolute about Muslim responsibility to 'put its own house in order'. Thus its first editorial after the 7/7 terrorist attack wove the paper's obsession with 'controlling our borders' into its anti-Blair stance:

> Are we losing the war on terror? Did our involvement in Iraq contribute to these attacks? Have we lost control of our borders, and does this make further attacks impossible to prevent? What nationality were the killers, and if any were British, can we prevent this country becoming a breeding ground for extremists? Is the leadership of the Metropolitan Police too concerned with ticking politically correct boxes to confront effectively the growing threat? Was there a failure of intelligence? Were the estimated £120 milllion spent on security at Gleneagles, and the 1,500 Metropolitan Police officers sent to Scotland, the best use of the available resources?

If I had read these editorials at the time, I would have strongly agreed with one sentiment, since it was what I was feeling painfully, too:

> Doesn't it beggar belief ... that when the G8 summit offered such an obvious opportunity for a terrorist 'spectacular' Britain's security level was downgraded? ... Didn't they think of vulnerable London before sending 1,500 Metropolitan Police to protect the summit?

The editorial of 9 July drew on a number of long-term *Mail* themes, including the war in Iraq. Two days later, it was the turn of the newspaper's strident policy that Labour is too weak on immigration and content with 'notoriously porous borders'. The piece attacked the government's 'incompetence [which] has left our immigration system in a shambles, with 570,000 foreign nationals living here illegally and our capital city such a centre for extremist groups that overseas intelligence services derisively describe it as "Londonistan"'. This was supported the following day in an article entitled 'US in Scathing Attack on "Londonistan"', quoting major American newspapers, as well as anti-terror experts, arguing that Britain's immigration and multicultural policy is weakening its heritage and providing asylum for terrorists who threaten both the UK and the US. The *Mail* was, though, also ready to be scathing about the US, with a piece by Max Hastings on 8 July describing a Britain, and a Blair, completely in thrall to the excesses of President Bush:

> Bush's bellicose rhetoric, his commitment to crude military might as a means of imposing his vision of US universalism on the world, form a huge obstacle to harmony to Western relations with Islam. It is hard to think of a US president so ignorant of the world, so insensitive to human behaviour, so

shameless in his pursuit of narrow, crude national interest as the current occupant of the White House.

In the *Mail*'s view, protecting ourselves from Bush's policy required three things urgently: the Metropolitan Police must stop its policy of 'hounding officers falsely accused of racism' since that 'political correctness may be blunting the Met's effectiveness'; senior judges must give less weight to human rights issues and stop trashing 'the Government's tough – though admittedly flawed – anti-terror laws'; and 'the mainstream Muslim community also has a vital part to play in fighting the evil in our midst . . . In the hunt for the terrorists, as Trevor Phillips of the Commission for Racial Equality says, there must be no weasel words about Iraq and Guantánamo Bay. These serial killers deserve no quarter.'

That Max Hastings' trenchant pieces appeared at that time in both the *Daily Mail* and the *Guardian* should make us pause before using the terms 'right' and 'left' too simplistically about this period. Finding itself attacking a Prime Minister whom many Tory politicians and voters see as a natural successor to Mrs Thatcher, the *Daily Mail* (like the *Sun*) was tying itself up in knots over issues of national, party and voter identity.

The issue of finding identity was as much a problem for some of our national newspapers as it was for me as I tried to rebuild my life after 7 July.

FIVE

22 July: The Killing of Jean Charles de Menezes

Late in the morning of 22 July I was on the phone to the bomb squad.

I had been talking with them in their various, developing manifestations since my early days in hospital. Initially this was because of my anxiety over my cabin bag, which had been whisked away with the clothes I was wearing during the explosion, and my watches, wallet and mobile phone, for police forensic analysis. I had been plaguing Ian, my police liaison officer, about this during all of my time in hospital, and he was always diligent and accommodating in trying to find out about them, despite it being out of his control. He took care to warn me that the forensic work must have priority and would take a long time.

By the time I left hospital, the bomb-squad team had begun to log the enormous number of items either found on the wrecked bus and trains or gathered from victims. Soon after I had got back to Janet's flat I was given the file number for two things, which I assumed to be my clothing and watches (recorded as twelve items) and what I thought was my cabin bag (recorded as one item), though this could not be confirmed. Over the coming days and then weeks, I started asking about my missing things from the train as well, especially my roller case and my laptop, which, if still intact, held my Ph.D. report for Teresita, my Colombian student. The case also held a copy of the report on floppy disk. I was supposed to be in Belfast examining the thesis (which I thought outstanding) on Monday, 25 July. My plane ticket was paid for, and Teresita's much more expensive ticket from Colombia was paid for, but without my presence as her external examiner or at the very least my written report, her journey would be wasted.

However, the inevitably painstaking work of the bomb squad was a bigger force than the bureaucracy of British universities. In the end the university sensibly compromised and allowed me to email a two-line overview, from my befuddled memory, of Teresita's Ph.D. thesis (this gained her an informal approval, which was then confirmed after my memory stick and report had turned up).

The bomb squad detectives kept visiting. In the last week of July – and supposedly the day of the Ph.D. viva in Belfast – two policemen came to the flat to check my DNA via a mouth swab. I asked whether I was now being considered a suspect. In a very relaxed fashion they concurred, and I began to feel sick. Soon after that, in early August, two detective constables arrived with my cabin bag and memory stick. Most things were in good order except for my grandfather's watch, and I eagerly signed the police form saying that I would take full responsibility for the items and for any unwanted hazards that might remain even after police cleaning.

Next, in mid-August, came the visit of DC Mark Denman with my shredded roller case and destroyed laptop. He had rung Janet some days before the visit, cautioning her to prepare me for it, given the awful state of the bags. He had worked among the horrendous destruction, despair and body parts for eight days in that tunnel near Edgware Road, and now he brought the roller case in a big black bin bag. No one touched the lacerated case itself as I peered into the plastic bag to see it. This was a look and goodbye situation, a form of closure, before he took the remains away with him. He left the laptop, hoping it might still work, even though its bag was also dreadfully damaged. In fact, when our technicians at work saw the laptop, they said they had never seen one so bad, even laptops that had fallen out of high buildings. It had imploded.

Then, on 7 October, exactly three months after the blast and in the midst of some unwanted media attention (which I'll describe later), a detective constable returned with my wrecked clothes and my shoes and belt. He advised me from the start that the clothes, though cleaned, neatly pressed and plastic-wrapped, would not be usable and would probably upset me. I took his advice and didn't look at them closely, and he took them away. The belt and strong (very new) leather shoes were in quite good condition, and I kept them – the right shoe, with its small shrapnel marks on the toe, to remind me of how lucky I had been.

After seeing the roller case, which had screened my feet and lower legs from the close blast, and the laptop bag, which must have protected my thighs, I felt immense, almost unbelieving, relief, and real fear, too. The explosion, Craig was the first to tell me, had been in my carriage and very, very close to me, and as I came to know this a feeling of extraordinary luck and at the same time a particular fear grew within me. I know that statistically it is highly unlikely for me to be exposed to a terrorist attack again, but statistics mean nothing to you if you have been hit before (when similar statistics applied). The natural feeling becomes, If that happens again, I couldn't be so lucky a second time.

These contacts with the bomb squad were all emotionally

draining for me. They left me feeling uneasily ambivalent, as, for example, the time I was on the phone to the bomb team asking about my missing shoes and I was read the full list of logged shoes, one with human parts attached. When I saw the terrible condition of my bags and clothes, I was left feeling horribly scared yet lucky.

There was joy at the return of my grandfather's watch (itself a bloodstained, burnt and scary sight, having been on my right wrist, three feet from the blast), the memory stick, my flat keys, my mobile (which contained most of my contact numbers, since my diaries had also been lost in the blast) and the redoubtable, black cabin bag itself, stained, as it still was, with dried blood from unknown sources.

When I made that call to the bomb squad on 22 July, I was already feeling anxious and emotionally ambivalent. As always, the police were patient, professional and friendly, doing their job in the right order of priorities – first the urgent forensic work, next the urgent, emotional support work with bereaved families (for example, taking them to the blast sites, helping them at all hours of the day and night), before the bureaucratic task of logging and returning items. That they did it all with sensitivity was something that struck me strongly through all my contacts with them.

I had called the team that morning because they had mentioned possibly returning some of my items (the Ph.D. examination on Monday, 25 July, was getting very close). However, the detective I spoke to said they had been held back from their routine work of logging and checking by the terrorist attacks of the day before, and that there had been another related incident that morning. I asked him what that incident was. Was it connected to the 21 July attack? He said it wasn't something he could speak about on the phone. That related incident was the shooting of Jean Charles de Menezes.

'One Down . . . Three to Go'

The *Sun* newspaper headline on 23 July was 'One Down . . . Three to Go'. It described the story of a 'Suspect shot dead', and, linking this 'SUICIDE bomb suspect' to the 'four men believed to be behind Thursday's attempted outrage', noted that the police had released CCTV pictures of these. The *Daily Mail*'s headline that day made the same connection, using the released CCTV images of the four suspects on its front page: 'Human Bombs. As SAS-Trained Marksmen Execute a Suspect on the Tube, the Desperate Hunt for these Suicide Bombers. Find Him: Shepherd's Bush Tube bomber. Find Him: Warren Street Tube bomber. Find Him: Shoreditch Bus Bomber. Find him: The Oval Tube bomber. Find Him.' The *Evening Standard* headline on the evening of 22 July stated as a truth, 'Bomber is Shot Dead on the Tube'.

By 25 July, the *Sun* recognised that there had been a mistake. Under the heading 'A Tragic Casualty of War', Andy McNab, '*Sun* Security Advisor and SAS Hero', wrote a piece explaining that in the 'harsh reality of life in London . . . we are at war', 'collateral damage' is inevitable and 'innocent people die'. But, echoing the newspaper's Blitz-style editorial of 8 July, McNab said these innocent people die 'so that the rest of us can live . . . We need to look at these sorts of tragic incidents with a new and tougher mentality, like how mindsets in the US hardened up after 9/11.' Examples of this tougher mentality are evident in the main story on that page of the *Sun*, 'Someone Else Will Get Shot', which quotes the Metropolitan Police Commissioner, Sir Ian Blair, insisting that the shoot-to-kill-to-protect policy would continue, and that he could not guarantee that 'other innocent people would not be shot by officers fearing another suicide bomb attack'. The same article quoted Tony Blair in support of the commissioner, accepting that 'more innocent people may be shot in attempts to stop suicide bombers'.

Hero Andy McNab helped circulate the myth at the time that Jean Charles de Menezes jumped over the ticket barrier after being confronted by the police security team: 'Would I have shot the Brazilian? You're damn right I would. I'd have probably killed him the moment he jumped over the station's ticket barrier.' For McNab, de Menezes was in the wrong place doing the wrong thing at the wrong time. He emphasised that, 'I want the firearms officer who shot the innocent man on Friday to know that he has my 110% support.'

The following day, *Sun* journalist Richard Littlejohn added a *Daily Mail*-type touch in his article 'Wrong Place. Wrong Time':

> It turns out that the Brazilian shot by the police on the Tube at Stockwell was almost certainly in the country illegally. Now why doesn't that surprise me? Jean Charles de Menezes came here on a student visa which expired two years ago. So he shouldn't have been here at all. There's some talk of a Portuguese passport but no-one's been able to produce it. Yes, it appears that he was working as an electrician. Was he qualified? Was he registered? Was he paying tax and National Insurance? On the face of it, Mr de Menezes would seem to be just one of the 570,000 illegal immigrants living in Britain the Government admits to knowing about. His immigration status would explain why he ran away from police and ignored repeated requests to surrender, even though his friends and family say he spoke perfect English. It obviously doesn't justify him being killed. But he was in the wrong place at the wrong time and undoubtedly contributed to his own death, tragic though it was.

In the *Mail* itself, however, this classic blaming-the-victim strategy was both moderated ('If, as police and witnesses say, Mr de Menezes was wearing a quilted jacket deemed suspicious on a warm day which might have concealed a suicide belt, why was he not stopped before boarding the bus?') and explained away, as in Melanie Phillips' piece 'A Terrible Tragedy – But This Is No Time For Weakness'. Phillips explains that the police 'reacted wrongly', though 'with great courage', because 'of an appalling lack of intelligence information', which has become systemic in Britain. In any case:

> The Metropolitan Police Commissioner, Sir Ian Blair, was right to insist that the instruction to shoot dead suspected ticking human bombs would remain. And he was right to warn that such terrible mistakes may happen again. But brutal realism must not stop there. It must also mean taking all necessary steps against all those who might harm us, including securing our borders, and it must mean radical improvements to intelligence. This country is facing an unprecedented type of war. We cannot fight it with our hands tied behind our backs.

To Phillips, anything less than this degree of 'brutal realism' would be 'appeasement' of the global assaults by Islamic fanatics.

On Tuesday, 26 July, however, in the same newspaper Stephen Glover countered the 'civilization clash' thesis of Phillips in his piece 'Am I Alone in Thinking That Pumping Seven Bullets into the Head of an Innocent Man is NEVER Justified?' He regrets that 'the prevailing view among newspapers, politicians, security experts, and, of course, the police [and] even among the liberal Left' is that de Menezes' death was an understandable accident, which could be repeated under the necessary 'shoot to kill' policy. Glover counters this at three levels. At the personal level:

> I wonder whether in their hearts most ordinary people will really defend what happened. An innocent man who was not

carrying a bomb or any other weapon, who lies helpless on the floor . . . is shot once in the mouth, six times in the head, and once in the shoulder. By a policeman.

At the level of legality:

The police themselves have devised new guidelines which they deem necessary to cope with new dangers. But they won't let us see those guidelines. They haven't been approved by Parliament. Indeed, as far as Parliament is concerned, we still live in a country whose police do not carry guns. In fact, a couple of thousand police in London carry them every day.

And at the level of democracy and the state:

Nasty states behave like that. Nasty states gun down their enemies in back streets rather than go to the trouble of bringing them to a court of law. Nasty states do not mind over-much if they bump off innocent people by mistake. We are not yet a nasty state, but we must do all we can to ensure that we do not become one . . . Last Friday was a dark day for this country. So, of course, was July 7. If we really are involved in a war of civilisations, let us be sure that our civilisation is not destroyed in the battle, so that we end up little better than those who wish to ruin it.

By 30 July, the *Mail* reporter Gordon Rayner was raising 'disturbing questions' in his piece 'Gunned-Down Brazilian Did NOT Vault Ticket Barrier and Was NOT Wearing a Winter Coat'. Under the headings 'Was He Given the Chance to Surrender?', 'Why Wasn't He Challenged as He Was Leaving His Flat?', 'Was He Wearing a Winter Coat?', 'Did he Vault the Barrier?', 'Did the Police Identify Themselves?', 'Was He Under Control When Shot?' and 'Was the Intelligence Flawed?'

Rayner was indeed raising worrying issues, and getting close to some of the right answers. As he noted, the police's confidential document 'Operation Kratos' states that a 'critical headshot' may be necessary 'prior to challenge', and despite Ian Blair's claim to the contrary, Jean Charles de Menezes was never challenged. Rayner asks, 'Why was he allowed to get on a bus near his home when buses had been targeted in the two previous bomb attacks?', and rightly surmises that the police did not know which flat he had emerged from. 'If he wore no heavy winter-coat, did the police have any reason to believe Mr de Menezes was a bomber – other than he looked foreign, lived in the block under surveillance, and used public transport?' Rayner also supposes, again probably rightly, that, as de Menezes did not vault the ticket barrier but used an Oyster card to go through, witnesses who reported he did jump the barrier were probably referring to plain-clothes police who were following him. And, though Rayner did not know it at the time of writing, the intelligence was certainly flawed, with the identification of the suspect having been made quickly by a soldier (who was not watching but relieving himself when de Menezes left the building) on the basis of a vague, individual feeling that he looked a bit like one of the suspects captured by CCTV cameras in the London Underground.

Other newspapers got to Rayner's disturbing questions a bit earlier. Thus the *Evening Standard*, despite its 'Bomber is Shot Dead on the Tube' headline on 22 July, was asking editorially its own serious questions just three days later:

> One is whether surveillance officers distinguished between the different tenants of the nine flats in the block they were watching. Another is whether a suspected suicide bomber should have been allowed to board a bus, which is no less a terrorist target than a Tube train. A third is whether the police clearly identified themselves as such in challenging Mr

de Menezes . . . Could he have been detained before boarding an Underground train? And, most pertinently, why was
he shot in the back of the head if he was prostrate on the
ground and apparently in no position to detonate an explo-
sive device?

Similarly, also on 25 July, the *Guardian* editorial, while generally supporting the police position, asked its 'unanswered
questions' (the first perhaps with Abu Ghraib in mind):

Was it a system failure or an individual at fault? It is usually
the former. How good was the intelligence and the analysis
that the officers carrying out the surveillance were receiving?
How many people who left the flats were also followed? Why
was Mr De Menezes suspected, apart from an inappropriate
winter coat? . . . If the police were worried by a possible
bomb attack on the tube, why were they not equally per-
turbed by one on the bus? On what grounds – and by
whom – were the officers following Mr Menezes given the
green light to proceed as though he was a terrorist? In precisely what form did the plain clothes police officers identify
themselves as police officers? Could they have been mistaken
by Mr De Menezes for terrorists? The tube station's cameras
may provide some answers to the last two questions.

But what is especially notable in all of this media coverage of
the killing of Jean Charles de Menezes is that, despite making
an immediate and false connection between him and the 21 July
bombers via the CCTV images of them in front-page photographs and headlines, these newspapers did not ask themselves
this: why were we not seeing CCTV images of Jean Charles de
Menezes at Stockwell Tube Station, as he supposedly leapt over
the ticket barrier and ran headlong down the escalator to the
train? No newspaper seemed to be questioning its own policy of

using artists' impressions mapping de Menezes' supposed actions at Stockwell that morning. Thus *The Times* published on 23 July an artist's detailed reconstruction of de Menezes going through the two levels of the station, with accompanying explanations: '1. Young man followed by two to three plain-clothes police into Stockwell station ticket hall. 2. He panics and runs, jumping the ticket barrier. 3. Police give chase down the escalator leading to the northbound platform. 4. He runs on to the Northern Line platform where a train has just arrived. 5. Police close in as he slips while trying to enter the train, and he is shot. 6. Victoria Line train pulls in. Passengers try to flee towards exits but are ordered back by station announcements. 7. Up to 20 armed police arrive and seal off the area.'

Indeed, some newspapers seem to have been taken in by their own artist's impressions (based on confused witnesses' reports) and even by some of their own unanswered questions, such as the *Evening Standard*'s point about the Brazilian being held prostrate on the floor of the train. The apparent precision and continuity of the details directed attention, mine included, towards trying to explain why he had run and fallen (despite his family saying that, having lived in São Paulo, where armed police tended to shoot people who ran, he would not have done so), and away from the causal plausibility of the police's claimed actions once they had arrived at Stockwell Station.

The *Daily Mail* editorial of 25 July said that Sir Ian Blair was 'surely . . . right to state unequivocally that his officers would continue to pursue a "shoot to kill" policy against suspected terrorists . . . And with four (at least) bombers still out there, nothing must fetter those charged with hunting them down'. On 30 July, the *Sun* carried the front-page headline 'Got the Bastards', with a photograph of one of the four captured suspects, enabling the newspaper to sweep under the carpet all of the accusations of police incompetence and the extra-legality in shooting Jean de Menezes. Similarly, the *Daily Mirror* headline

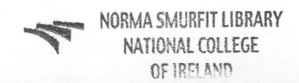

on that day was, 'Got Them', with a photo of two of the arrested suspects on their balcony in north Kensington, and the editorial commented:

> If ever there was complete justification for saying that we have the greatest force in the world, it was yesterday. If ever the British people felt they could breathe more easily because of their police, it was yesterday . . . With a bit of help from their Italian colleagues, that is entirely thanks to the police. Sadly their 'best day ever' coincided with the funeral of the Brazilian boy shot by mistake. Nothing can bring him back and his family is entitled to every sympathy. But the triple triumph of yesterday, following the other capture earlier in the week, shows the true face of the British police.

And so, Jean Charles de Menezes was twice buried that day. Once in the ground back home in Brazil, and also in a British media frenzy of praise for the 'greatest force in the world'. For me, though, and for many others I'm sure, there began a fear of being killed on public transport by people other than terrorists. Given that, according to the *Mail*'s Gordon Rayner, Kratos police indicators of the 'behaviour of a suicide bomber' include 'Sweating . . . Looking anxious. Holding something in the hand/clenched fist', I knew that when I finally got back on the Tube, especially between Edgware Road and Paddington, I would be doing all of those things. As de Menezes' cousin Matheus Sanchez wrote in the *Evening Standard* on 25 July, 'If they kill someone like my cousin Jean then everyone should be afraid.'

I usually found good sense on these complicated issues in the columns of *Guardian* journalist Peter Preston, whose comments will appear again later in this book. In his article 'Stockwell is Not the Place for a Soapbox', he notes the 'catalogue of certainties' the public has been given through the media, from

WMD to the killing of de Menezes to Sir Ian Blair saying he could trace a direct link between the Brazilian and the bombers. As for the media's own responses to the de Menezes killing:

> We denizens of Pundit Towers are no better. Did you like the *Telegraph*'s 'Ten urgent steps to make Britain safer'? ... Step one: 'Confidently assert British values'; two, 'Exclude foreign undesirables'; three, 'Repeal the Human Rights Act'. Not to mention step seven, the one they called 'Sensible policing'. Sensible? 'Sensitivity, in today's context, is a policy of wilfully ignoring the individuals most likely to be terrorists. In the face of the threat of terrorism, we must all accept an impact on the way we live.' *Telegraph* leader writers are not alone to be sure. The blood and glass had barely been cleared from Tavistock Square before Melanie Phillips was turning her *Mail* guns on a Britain so terrified of being accused of Islamophobia that it had 'paid the ultimate and terrible price'. All hail America, apparently, which has 'draconian border controls – including racial and religious profiling – which enables officials to stop people if they correspond to certain suspect characteristics . . . Media pundits of any persuasion are supposed to come up with steaming theses before breakfast. But, just one dead Brazilian electrician later, there's a codicil to add. Uncertainty – simple, inevitable fallibility – isn't a crime. It's the human condition. What do suicide bombers do when the police have them cornered? In Madrid, one blew himself and the arresting officer up. Naturally, that makes police officers edgy. The real answer, time and again, start to finish, in this dismal affair, is 'Don't know'.

Preston's point about uncertainty is well taken, but it is also a prescription for letting those who say they have to act – like armed police, or prime ministers on the edge of a war with Iraq – off the hook. And sometimes it is the less prestigious local media that ask the crucial questions about 'Who's Calling the Shots?', which was the title of the editorial in my local paper, the *Camden New Journal*, on 28 July:

> Bearing in mind that Britain is a democracy where the elected politicians govern, and civil servants, including the police, carry out their policies, we can only hope that if a 'shoot to kill policy' exists it was approved by the Home Secretary. Here lies the mystery. From the Prime Minister and the Home Secretary there is tight-lipped silence. No recognition that such a policy throws into relief grave constitutional questions.

The Camden paper accused the media of 'hysterical knee-jerk reactions' over the killing of an innocent man but complete silence on the legality of the shoot-to-kill policy. De Menezes' lawyer, speaking at a public meeting, was the only person to mention this. In the absence of words on the matter from the media, and in the face of 'silence from cowering politicians', the *Camden New Journal* asked, 'Who is running Britain?'

Following the line of Camden's local newspaper, I'll finish this chapter by asking my own 'Who's Calling the Shots?' question. Given all the detail we received as to why shooting in the head was necessary in the age of terrorism, and given the rhetoric of some British newspapers calling for brutal realism in a country 'facing an unprecedented type of war', why did we read in the *Independent* on 25 October, above a picture of Jean Charles de Mcnezes, that 'Police are given shoot-to-kill powers in domestic violence and stalking cases'? We are, of course, assured by 'one of the country's most senior police chiefs' that 'the decision to shoot a suspect in the head would only be used under exceptional circumstances' in cases of stalking, blackmail and domestic violence.

Just tell that to the family of Jean Charles de Menezes. The creeping spread of this undemocratic shoot-to-kill policy was only one example of my growing concerns over Britain's burgeoning culture of fear and threats to civil liberties. This was to come to a very visible parliamentary confrontation in November, when the *Sun* used my photo to support Tony Blair's anti-terror legislation.

SIX

Engaging the Media

On Sunday, 24 July, in the midst of the turmoil over the attacks, my two sons, Anton and Rowan, flew into Heathrow from Australia to help me with my recuperation.

The Australian federal government, through its Centrelink organisation, was financially supporting direct family visits to Australian victims of the bombings, for which I was very grateful. Nonetheless, I had not expected everything to be in such a state of nervous unrest in London when they had booked their flights one week before.

For many people, both in London and in the regions of Britain as well, 21 July marked a time, as Mark Lawson had written the day before my sons arrived, of a 'Tube dread felt deeper'. Personal friends were emailing me and saying how nervous they were of visiting me in London. From Janet's flat I had heard the police action at Warren Street, and I had been terribly disturbed by the killing of Jean Charles de Menezes. So there was plenty of anxiety in my mind on 24 July, when Teresa from the Australian High Commission and Lou, the Australian Centrelink social worker, met Anton and Rowan at the airport, and brought them to their hotel halfway between Warren Street Station and Janet's place in Camden Town.

When they arrived at the flat that morning, tired from a fairly sleepless twenty-three-hour flight, I told them what had been developing while they were in the air. I gave them the precautionary advice about travelling which Lou had given me the day before. Basically she had said to tell them it was all right to feel nervous when travelling, to follow their instincts, and if they felt anxious in the company of another passenger either to change carriage or to get off the train straight away. They both took this advice, and also decided not to travel by Tube or bus in London during their visit.

As part of the strategy I had learned from my physio Maggie and my occupational therapist Erin, Anton and Rowan were allocated a particular and important role in helping me achieve small targets. Only a few days earlier, I had begun to feel confident in my balance, moving around Janet's flat – the incident with her grandson William's little yellow chair helped a lot – and feeling more stable when being showered by my carers. I reckoned it was time to venture outside properly, and on the morning Anton and Rowan arrived Janet set the task of walking me along the busy Hampstead Road to a new Mexican restaurant. Both my sons like good food, especially hot food, so I knew I would be going to restaurants with them if I could manage. It was one thing I could offer them, apart from my uncertain company, for giving up a week of their very busy time – Rowan was in the late stages of his Ph.D. on computer games at the University of New South Wales and Anton was taking time off from his job in IT at Unisys in Sydney.

The walk to the restaurant was about two hundred metres, and although Sunday mornings are relatively quiet on the Hampstead Road, I was enormously pleased I managed it. That seemed to me light years of improvement beyond my sitting at the bus stop, and it had a pleasant purpose as well. Next, my sons were set two specific targets: to try to get me into vehicles (but not buses or Underground trains) to go to restaurants if we couldn't walk there, and to extend my outdoor walking, with the target of a thirty-minute each-way walk from the flat to the lake at Regent's Park.

We managed both. We went to restaurants in London – Indian, Nepalese and Mexican – usually by taxi, after detailed explanations of vertigo to taxi drivers: 'Please slow down for speed bumps' (of which there seem to be millions in London's backstreets – especially around Janet's flat) and, 'Please avoid fast right or left turns.' And so we did that, most evenings. Taxi drivers were enormously friendly and supportive. Although there was one time, after we had been to one of our old favourites among London's Indian restaurants, the Red Fort in Dean Street, when I didn't warn the taxi driver. I paid the penalty when he hit a speed bump at what seemed like 40 mph, and I bounced up in the air, with unpleasant results.

That week I was wearing a hearing aid I had been lent by the audiology technician at St Mary's. It wasn't a decent fit, and constantly made loud whistling noises. At one of our meals out, Anton demonstrated the effect this might be having on the ambience for other diners, by slowly walking backwards from the table until he couldn't hear it – about twenty metres. He was worried anyway at the effect it might be having on my repairing eardrums.

I had been for a test and check-up on my ears at St Mary's on 20 July – strapped flat-out in an ambulance – and had been given hopeful advice from the specialist there, who said that my right ear was showing good signs of repair, while the left was showing a bit of improvement. (On 3 August, at my next visit, to a different specialist, I was given contrary advice: there was no sign of repair at all. Bearing in mind that this was in the crucial four-to-six-week period when, so I had been told in hospital, the 90 per cent chance of self-repair should be showing up, that left me as down as I had been since the attacks.)

The trips outside with Anton and Rowan were making me feel I was getting back to normal. There were all the taxi rides sitting upright so I would feel confident to sit up in the ambulance on 3 August. There was also my first train journey since the blast, which we planned for Saturday, 30 July, to Brighton. A *Doctor Who* exhibition was being held at Brighton Pier, and as all three of us are long-term fans of the programme and especially liked the 2005 series, the idea seemed perfect for a family travelling exercise.

There was a lot of detailed preparation for it. Erin discussed with me my vertigo and nausea in relation to trains. She emphasised that there were two types of train I could use to get to Brighton. One was the fast train, first stop East Croydon. This would take less time, but what if I began to feel nauseous straight away, with the first stop twenty minutes away? Alternatively, I could get the much slower stopping train, but it was likely to be more of a rattle trap. This was the kind of meticulous planning we did for every campaign into the outside world, especially when travelling by public transport. Anton and Rowan were warned to have a strategy prepared in case we had to get off the train because of my sickness, since I couldn't be left alone and Janet wouldn't be there (she is not a fan of *Doctor Who*). Also, Erin said, I should think about where I sat on the train: 'Don't sit next to the window,' she said, as the effect of seeing things flashing by close up would likely be nauseous. 'Try to keep looking straight down the centre of the carriage.'

The great expedition began that Saturday. On the way to Victoria Station, we dropped into the family support centre, which my new police liaison officer had told me about earlier in the week. It was a great set-up in Vincent Hall, with helpful social workers who gave me advice on how to apply to the London Bomb Relief Fund, and a travel officer who gave me an Oyster card to allow free travel on London buses and Underground trains for a month (which I appreciated, but didn't plan to be using much).

It felt like I was going through real but tumultuous progress during this week, travelling and meeting all these people outside the flat. Still, the train to Brighton was going to be a big test. It was my first train trip since the bombing.

I was very taken aback by all the backpacks piled up in every carriage, and had one right next to me for the whole journey. It was hard to keep my eyes off it, but at least that kept them from straying out of the windows. We had decided to risk the fast train, and that worked very well, with my only attack of nausea as we approached Brighton through the Downs, trees flashing by close on either side. I couldn't avoid seeing them, even staring straight down the carriage, and began to feel sick. When we got to the station, this necessitated a change of plan. I had intended for us to take a taxi to the pier, but was feeling too sick to deal with the extra motion. We walked down the hill, the mile or so to the pier. The next encounter was a test, too: my first time mixing with large crowds of people, in a hot indoor centre. It was quite claustrophobic, but a good show which we enjoyed. Afterwards, we walked all the way back uphill to Brighton Station; a very long walk for me, but even more of a hassle for Anton, who was carrying my huge and rather heavy Tardis biscuit jar. I recall him mentioning that he was beginning to feel a mite irritated that I was regaining an earlier tendency to leave him behind as we walked, especially now he was carrying the Tardis.

I had prepared for that longer walk the day before. Friday was the day I had decided on for my walk to Regent's Park. Rowan was visiting relatives, so it was a job for Anton and me. Janet had listened to Erin and gave me detailed strategic advice for the journey: there were no seats in the twenty-minute walk to the edge of the park, but there was a low wall I could rest on at a bus stop. And Anton must have been listening in turn to Janet because on the way back through the park, after a cup of coffee at the lakeside restaurant – and at a moment when I was steaming along feeling very pleased with myself – he pointed out the last seat before the park limits, and asked if I needed a rest. Little things like this – a walk, a bit of unexpected advice from my son – made me feel very good. Indeed, strolling through the Regent's Park rose garden was a revelation to me. For the first time since the explosion, I could walk and look around at the lovely, scented flowers, without fearing the visual impact that cars or people flashing by might have. At that moment I valued my life in a way I never had before. Turning my head around for the first time since 7 July to look at the roses, walking, talking with my son Anton, felt like a kind of epiphany, washing away some of the death and horror of carriage two at Edgware Road.

The week was one of great recuperation and progress, which I owed to my sons and the Australian government that had sent them over. It was also a week in which Anton and Rowan began to take on a second, key role as I decided to try taking a more active approach to my image in the media. Partly, this was the result of a growing sense of control over my own body; partly, it was to do with my natural curiosity as a media academic; and partly, my simmering political emotions were calling for more cognitive engagement.

Talking with the media

Ever since 8 July, when St Mary's and my hospital ward were invaded by Aussie journalists, I had been aware that my picture was going to get into newspapers. But neither I nor my family was ready for the sheer amount of exposure. As a partner in the 'Coalition of the Willing' in Iraq with Britain and the US, Australia had a keen interest in the events of 7 July, and the media there began to feature images of Australian survivors, including of me, ascribed (as in the photo with Prince Charles) and non-ascribed (as in the shot of me at Edgware Road over the Union Jack and London Underground logo behind the TV news readers on Channel 9). Rupert Murdoch's newspaper *The Australian* carried a picture of me shaking hands cheerfully with Prince Charles in its weekend edition on 9–10 July, under the headline 'Allies Unite Against Terror'. The New South Wales broadsheet daily, the *Sydney Morning Herald*, carried the first full-body shot of me (labelled, 'Shattered . . . an injured man is led from Edgware Road Tube Station') in a big colour photo on 8 July, next to the headline 'Dreaded Strike Turns Into Reality'. The Sydney tabloids, the *Sun Herald* and the *Sunday Telegraph* – whose journalist (the 'friend' with the pot plant) had visited me at St Mary's, taking close-up head shots – carried hospital pictures of me and other Australian survivors, under headlines like 'Unbowed Britain', 'Caught in the Horror', 'A Leather Jacket, a Sense of Humour – The Stuff of Miracles' and 'My Miracle Escape'. The regional press quickly got in on the act, too, with the *Sunshine Coast Daily* carrying the Prince Charles photo of me under the heading 'The fateful morning I became one of London's living dead', and Bathurst's *Western Advocate* (the town where the Charles Sturt University campus I had worked at is located) carried the photo of me with Prince Charles under the heading 'John helped by a ministering angel. Prince Charles consoles former CSU academic after London bombing'. (The local media's appropriation of my image was one of the amusing aspects of all this – some Welsh media, for example, insisted on calling me a 'Welsh professor'.)

The glut of images continued for a week, especially after the St Mary's PR team invited Channel 9 and AAP to a bedside briefing before I left hospital. My family (and lots of emails from Australian friends) complained that my image seemed ubiquitous on television, with a particular bit of my talk with Prince

Charles about 'phoning back to Australia' being used as a promo for coming news events. I think it was all a bit too much for my anxious family, especially when one of Sydney's commercial TV channels approached Anton and Rowan to appear on a morning show to say how they felt. They politely declined this opportunity and a number of other TV and newspaper people asking for information and comments.

Much the same was happening, of course, in the UK, so that by the time Anton and Rowan arrived in London we needed to talk about a strategy for action. Rowan is a media/cultural studies scholar and Anton is pretty media savvy, so we formed a knowledgeable, but at this stage fairly media-helpless team. What was to be done in the face of this glut of media attention?

For probably the first time in my life, Anton and Rowan became my mentors and advisers. (It is a bit sad that you have to go through a near-death experience to achieve that, but I found it very welcome.) Their first advice was to avoid the Australian commercial media (there were plenty of requests for interviews coming in), on the grounds that they were peddling such simple 'moderate versus extremist Islam' anti-terrorist campaigns that it would be difficult to deal with their inevitable question, 'How angry do you feel?' without being trapped by culturally crude notions of mindless and mad fanatics (or even risk being labelled a terrorist-lover). At this stage, then, I was cautious about appearing in the more tabloid media.

To some extent I had already taken precautionary action, as had the press office at St Mary's, by not giving Janet's address or telephone number to anybody, including family and work, in order to avoid doorstepping by the media. The Australian High Commission told me that one of the reasons for the Australian Prime Minister not paying me a visit that week, was that with his huge entourage it would be impossible to keep my address secret from the media. However, the net result was that the head of school's secretary at Brunel University, Mary, was getting inundated with media requests for interviews, which she was loyally passing on by email. So the issue still had to be faced.

In any case, I wanted some media access, because I had my own story to tell – which was not that of the innocent good guy hideously attacked by mindless Muslims. With Anton and Rowan, I began to sift through the possible contenders that might allow me to say a little bit more and combine personal, professional and political observations.

Channel 5 – '7/7: Attack on London'

I had recently been approached via email by Edwina Silver of Mentorn Films, who were planning a documentary, to be screened in September, on the terrorist attacks. On the phone, Edwina explained that her concept was one day in the life of London, running from the euphoria of London's Olympic bid success on the evening of 6 July to the horror of the terrorist attack, which everyone knew about by the evening of 7 July. My points to Edwina on the phone were twofold. First, I thought for many people the experiences after the bombings (including those with the media) might be more interesting. This was always going to be a documentary based on interviews with the victims at the four bomb sites, and not all of these would have been especially exercised by the Olympic story. In my own case, I remembered the night we heard that Sydney had got the 2000 Olympics. I had been in a motel room in rural Wagga Wagga in New South Wales surrounded by all the late-night fireworks, drinking and cheering. That had been 'my Olympics', and what I had seen of those games was a wonderful coming together of athletes, spectators, voluntary helpers and some really innovative TV programming. It was a bit harder on the night of 6 July 2005 for me to get quite so highly involved (even if, as Ken Livingstone has since promised, all the seriously injured are to be offered ringside seats for the London Olympics).

Obviously that was just an idiosyncratic caveat. My other, more important point to Edwina was that I would like my interview contribution to extend to a bit more than that of an innocent victim. In other words, there were some wider issues I would like to respond to. She said she would think about all this and contacted me again the day after Anton and Rowan arrived in London. She liked my idea of extending the concept of the programme beyond 7 July, and would be happy to talk with me about my wider thoughts face to face. A meeting was arranged for lunchtime in the foyer of Anton and Rowan's Thistle hotel (so that I didn't have media coming to the flat, and so that Anton and Rowan could easily be present). I warned that the meeting could be difficult because of my deafness and nausea; the day before I'd vomited quite a lot after the bomb squad police came to talk to me and administer mouth swabs to rule me out as a terror suspect.

On the day, 26 July, we talked at the hotel for about an hour. It went fine. I liked Edwina; she responded to my ideas, though she emphasised, fairly, that the production could not guarantee that everything I said would be aired. We all knew that anyway, but we wondered what principles guiding inclusion and exclusion might be in place. After Edwina left, Anton and Rowan said they thought I should not expect anything political to be kept in the documentary. Nonetheless, I liked Edwina's style, and was interested professionally to see just what I would get away with. It was a chance to be the kind of media academic I like to be, on the inside of a production.

A while later, Edwina, with her PA, sound man and cameraman, became the first media unit invited to Janet's sanctuary. The shooting took about three hours in the sitting room, with Janet banished to her study and prevented by the sound man from even making phone calls. It was an exhausting experience for me. I had to hold a sitting position for long periods, which was very hard given my vertigo. Also, the bright TV lights began to remind me of that yellow-light image in the train. I was sweating, whether through recall anxiety or just the heat of the lights, I don't know. The interview was structured, and towards the end Edwina offered the cue of a question linking my feelings of anger to things wider than the actual terrorists. By then, I was feeling pretty worn out and wanting it to be over, so I gave a shorter and more muted account of my feelings on Iraq and terrorism than I had planned. But it was an okay performance, I think, just a bit more low key and cautious.

When the programme went to air on 15 September on Channel 5 at 9 p.m., I sat down with some trepidation. In our meeting at the Thistle hotel Edwina had warned me that there might be some unpleasant images and descriptions of horrible injuries. I'd been talking to her about the two American women I remembered in the train, and she had got hold of some internet material on their condition, which had come from a military hospital in the US. The two women were actually sisters from Tennessee, who had met up in London for a holiday after a service programme in Kenya. The account of their injuries had upset me, and when Edwina became aware of that she mentioned that Mentorn might also be using the graphic personal account of the scene in that carriage by a *Daily Telegraph* journalist, who, like Craig Staniforth, had jumped into the train to help. At least three times before the screening, Mentorn personnel rang the flat to advise Janet that I should either watch the documentary in company or record it and fast-forward through any problem bits. I appreciated their sensitivity, and on 15 September sat down to watch the show with Janet. As I waited for the programme to come on, I felt anxious for another reason, too: this was my first attempt to project a slightly different image – as both citizen and professional – beyond that of helpless victim.

The documentary was tight, good entertainment and very professional. It began with an extended sequence using reconstructions and some actual CCTV footage to describe the journey of the three bad guys by car from Yorkshire in the early morning dark, their meeting with the fourth terrorist in the car park at Luton Station and their journey on the train to London King's Cross. It showed how they then fanned out in different directions, with one of them disconcerted to find the Northern Line closed, before wandering around disoriented and then boarding the fateful No. 30 bus. The following sequences covered in turn: the Edgware Road bombing, with me featuring prominently as I unknowingly got closer and closer to Mohammad Sidique Khan; the Aldgate bombing, with the national ballroom dancer, Bruce Lait, giving a graphic, moving account of the dead and dying bodies hurled across his legs and feet and his partner's body by the blast; the Russell Square Tube bombing, featuring a terribly shocked woman, Hazel Schewls, who clearly still found it hard to breathe as a result of post-traumatic stress; the Tavistock Square bus bombing, featuring the Australian woman, Louise Barry, who had terrible back and head injuries, and was still wearing a brace; and the poignant account of John Faulding, who lost his Israeli girlfriend on the bus. Finally, there was a reprise section about the victims 'now'.

My initial response to the documentary was, Where is my account of Craig Staniforth? Later in the programme, I understood the reason. Craig had declined to appear on the show, whereas in contrast a young American academic who had helped Louise Barry at Tavistock Square did appear extensively. The editing style was to cut from the Australian victim to the American helper, matching accounts almost word for word, and gaining the frisson of slight variation and different perspectives coming together. Radio Five Live later got a similar effect from a radio interview they did with Craig and myself for a transmission on 7 October. But in the documentary, with Craig

7 July 2005: from Edgware Road Tube Station to the world's media; first images of emergency-service workers helping me after the attacks. *(bigpicturesphoto.com)*

Another iconic image from Edgware Road – Davinia Turrell helped away from the horror by Paul Dadge. *(Rex Features)*

Tony Blair, at the G8 summit in Gleneagles, after hearing about the bombings. *(Gareth Fuller / PA)*

Early morning, 7 July: CCTV of Hasib Hussain, Germaine Lindsay, Mohammad Sidique Khan and Shehzad Tanweer entering Luton Station on the way to London. *(Rex Features)*

The destroyed second carriage of the Edgware Road Tube train. *(Rex Features)*

A mobile-phone image that brought back memories of the surreal contrasts after the explosion.

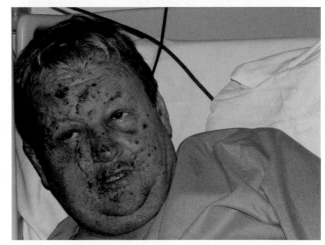

Groggy and concussed in St Mary's, 9 July. *(Gerhard Kiesenhofer)*

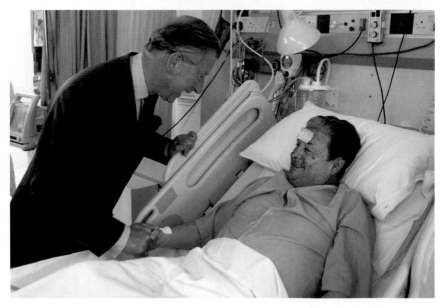

Prince Charles visits me in hospital, 8 July. *(Rex Features)*

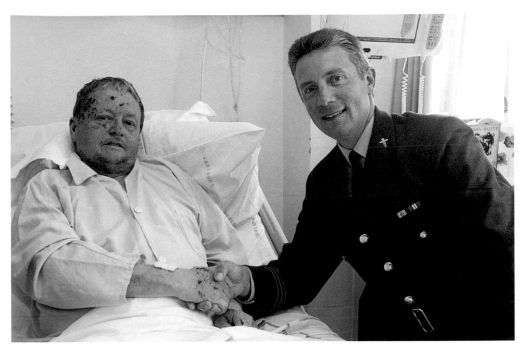

Reunited with Craig Staniforth, care of the *Sun*, 13 July. *(Sun)*

August 2005: Janet in her Camden flat, my place of recovery in the weeks that followed.

(John Tulloch)

Jean Charles de Menezes and
the would-be bomber he was
mistaken for, Hussain Osman.

(Rex Features)

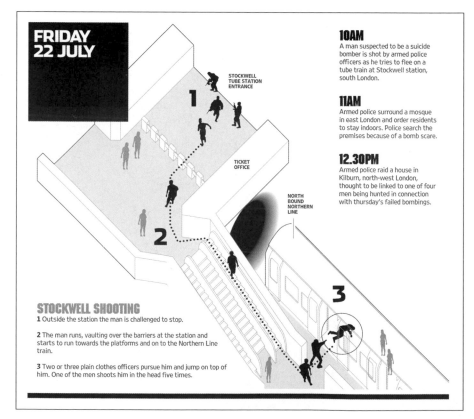

**FRIDAY
22 JULY**

STOCKWELL
TUBE STATION
ENTRANCE

1

TICKET
OFFICE

NORTH
BOUND
NORTHERN
LINE

2

3

10AM
A man suspected to be a suicide
bomber is shot by armed police
officers as he tries to flee on a
tube train at Stockwell station,
south London.

11AM
Armed police surround a mosque
in east London and order residents
to stay indoors. Police search the
premises because of a bomb scare.

12.30PM
Armed police raid a house in
Kilburn, north-west London,
thought to be linked to one of four
men being hunted in connection
with thursday's failed bombings.

STOCKWELL SHOOTING
1 Outside the station the man is challenged to stop.

2 The man runs, vaulting over the barriers at the station and
starts to run towards the platforms and on to the Northern Line
train.

3 Two or three plain clothes officers pursue him and jump on top of
him. One of the men shoots him in the head five times.

The *Observer*'s graphic on 24 July of de Menezes' supposed movements before
he was shot dead. *(Michael Agar / Cath Levett / copyright Guardian Newspapers Limited 2005)*

April 2003: Mohammad Sidique Khan as teaching assistant at Hillside Primary School.
(Joan Russell / Guzelian)

A still from an al-Jazeera videotape of Khan, released 1 September 2005. *(Rex Features)*

November 2005, working on the book in Australia . . . *(Adam Hollingsworth)*

. . . while the *Sun* cover
story broke in Britain.
(Guardian Newspapers Limited 2005)

absent, the Mentorn team had obviously dropped my comments about him.

As the drama unfolded, my next response was, Could I survive the bad bits? Janet was watching me as closely as the screen,
but I felt okay. Bruce's mention of a woman's dying body twitching on his legs, before emitting a huge gush of blood, was a bit
hard to take, and the American academic seemed to be going
into a bit too much lurid detail for me. But I did get through it,
unedited, in one go. As it was my first televisual encounter with
the major details of that awful day, I was worried, as I'm sure
the Mentorn team were, about the possibility of post-trauma
flashbacks. But they didn't happen.

My third response was to the reprise sequence of the documentary. This had a strong 'injured victim' signature. There was
Hazel, who couldn't breathe easily, saying she was frightened to
leave her flat now. There was Bruce, looking a bit shell-shocked
and saying twice that being trapped with the woman's body on
his legs 'wasn't very nice'. Then Louise, still constrained very
badly by her neck brace. And John talking about his lost partner,
showing, as the editor mentioned to me on the phone while she
was working on it close-up, deep and caring emotion despite his
apparent facial impassivity. And there was me. They had chosen
a prolonged shot when I wasn't speaking, but was displaying
facial twitches, some of which I've had since early childhood.
Initially I was sorry it ended that way, because, as my sons had
predicted, all my efforts to go on to wider issues had come to
naught. Rather than speaking with intent, as I had tried to do at
the end of the interview, in the finale of the programme I was
deprived of my words altogether, an innocent, twitching victim
of the bad guys (about whom the documentary had not given
any other context *except* as bad guys). So I was sorry, and a
number of academic friends emailed me straight after the show
with the same view about the ending.

In reality I had no reason to be annoyed. I have done enough work as an academic on television production from the inside, and have sufficient awareness of the importance of narrative, drama and genre, to know that the documentary succeeded very well indeed in its goals, which were to provide a gripping, tightly structured narrative with built-in, momentary cliffhangers (like my words, in close-up, 'And then . . . it happened' being edited into two, and a threatening shot of trains tearing down red-lit tunnels in the middle). This was a show for peak-time viewing, and it pulled out all the stops of human interest and tragedy, suspense, contrast of bomb sites and perspectives, good and evil and, finally, narrative closure around the victims. They did it very well, and it was a learning experience for me about engaging with the media. I phoned Anton and Rowan, who were by now back in Australia, to say they had been right in one sense, but that it was worth doing anyway.

Radio 4's *Today* programme

While Anton and Rowan were still in the UK, Radio 4's *Today* programme approached me. They were looking to do a 'one month on' discussion with a victim of the attacks to go out on 7 August, and I agreed to record it. The interview was with John Humphrys – him at home, me in Janet's flat – and a young producer, who would look after the mike and the timing. *Today* is a very professional, often critical and high-impact programme, with decision-makers, including politicians, appearing regularly. This seemed a good forum for me to speak about wider issues.

And I did, talking a fair bit about the effect of Iraq, and my anger therefore not so much with individual terrorists, but with the bigger picture behind their actions and those of our militaries doing less than good in Iraq. I also spoke a lot about my experience of the actual bombing, and I found John Humphrys a good listener and facilitator of what I had to say. The interview lasted about twenty-two minutes, and the producer said it was 'great, moving', and that it would appear at the weekend, edited down to seven or eight minutes. Later, she rang me to say that because there was a jointly controlled French/British theme on 'Brits in Brittany' on the Saturday, there might not be space for my interview then, in which case it would definitely appear on the Monday. I listened with expectation on both mornings, but there was no sign of the interview on either, though there was a punchy interview with George Galloway on Iraq on the Monday, which was responded to by the familiarly asinine polispeak of leading Conservative politician Liam Fox complaining that Galloway had twisted and manipulated history.

I was surprised they had not played the interview, given that the producer had said it was just what she wanted and that they would like to use me again on Iraq discussions. When I rang her on her way to work on the Tuesday, she seemed embarrassed and said she wasn't sure what was happening and, bluntly, that she could not release the edited tape to me. I discussed this by email with Anton and Rowan, now back in Australia, and we decided that if it had been a powerful discussion, as the producer had intimated, then maybe they felt it needed balancing (they had talked about getting a response from a Cabinet Minister or politician), or maybe they had just decided to replace it with the opposing views offered by Galloway and Fox.

If this was the case, I found it a bit depressing, given the reputation of *Today*. However, only days later I was emailed by a different *Today* producer, acknowledging the earlier interview and asking whether we could try again, given the currency of the Mohammad Sidique Khan video, which had just been released by al-Jazeera and shown on British TV. I was wary about doing this second interview for three reasons: first, I hadn't then seen the Khan video; second, it seemed like a major opportunity for a 'mad terrorist', 'ungrateful immigrant' inter-view, in which I would probably have no chance (just as Galloway didn't) to respond to the balancing interviewee; and thirdly, I was very down after my recent visit to the audiology specialist at St Mary's on 3 August, and didn't think in the cir-cumstances I would perform too well on complex issues.

My specialist consultant and audiology professor at St Mary's had checked my ears the day before, and had told me that the earlier specialist who said there were signs of progress had 'stuffed up' and had even got the drawings of my two eardrums the wrong way round. My ears were not improving, and after a further check a month later I was probably looking down the barrel of an operation. This was the first time since my sudden awareness of vertigo on 8 July that I had to deal with negative information about my progress, and it was exacerbated by the apparent disagreement among the specialists. All of my medical and social care support had been so outstanding that this came as a real surprise, a real downer that left me depressed for quite some time.

However, the Radio 4 producer was persistent, and on Friday, 5 August, I was facing another *Today* interviewer in Janet's flat. I was feeling far from performative. At the time Janet had a friend, Diana, visiting from Canada and I was tetchy and diffi-cult with both of them. They remained patient and supportive, and eased me into the interview in the study. It went well, and was edited even better by the *Today* people, going to air on Monday, 8 August, in a five-minute slot at about 7.50 a.m. Remembering how down and stressed I was on the day of the interview, I was surprised at how articulate I sounded.

I spoke about how I was 'remapping my reality' in the wrecked train carriage; how I shifted from survivor to victim mode with Craig; and how my recovery was a matter of very small, but to me very significant, moves, like the fact that the very morning of the interview I had stood up in the shower for the first time since the blast, and had walked with Anton for two half-hour stretches the previous Friday. Then the interviewer asked me the question, Why did I think it happened? This was the opening I had been waiting for. I said:

> I do think that it is linked to Iraq. I do think that politicians have deliberately over-simplified the arguments of people who say it is connected to Iraq. It is not simply that Iraq happened and then, like a billiard ball, this happened. Iraq actually means lots of different things . . . It has, for example, the meaning among an awful lot of people of an illegal war fought by a presidential-style leader who doesn't actually believe in popular democracy at all. Lots of people think about Iraq in moral terms, about Abu Ghraib and the despicable morality which reminds us too closely of Saddam Hussein. There is the Iraq that means, to a lot of people, Fallujah, and the killings of thousands upon thousands of harmless people, and when I got the force of that explosion and lay in hospital in pain for many days, I was getting just a touch of that sense and emotion and feeling and pain that these people have to face every day. What I'm saying is that Iraq is not simply something that happened that generates terrorists. It's a whole rhetorical set of meanings that won't go away. The Prime Minister may want to 'move on'. It's too symbolic, it's deep in our consciousness. There's me as a comfortably off, white, western, Australian/British citizen talking, and we know that millions of British people have a mix of those sorts of feelings about Iraq, and many more that they would tell us about. If you add to that the injustices that Muslim people have in this society, following their family histories, following their parents who worked hard and were spat on, people who get herded by the police and so on. I can't speak for them, they must speak for themselves. I am saying, though, that there's a huge alienation [across British society].

The interviewer then intervened by asking whether the terrorist attack wasn't a much more complicated matter than just Iraq, and I concluded with:

> The various meanings I was talking about, the various discourses about Iraq of course are more complicated than Iraq. Iraq is part of a much bigger picture, whether it's emotional, ideological, psychological, cultural – I mean, there's a whole range of things that are broader than Iraq. But what Iraq is doing is symbolising an awful lot that's wrong about how we relate internationally, and how we relate internally and domestically.

The interview got wide exposure, including in Australia, and colleagues and my sons contacted me to say that they liked it. From David in California, I got the email, 'I write to wish you a speedy recovery from your injuries and to thank you for such well-thought comments on the Iraq connection to terrorist acts.' My colleague Christina wrote, 'I heard you this morning early on the radio . . . I agreed with all you said. And it was good to hear that you're up and about and (I trust) feeling a good deal better.' From Mary, another academic in Plymouth, I got the email, 'I hope you will not mind a complete stranger contacting you . . . I found the lucidity and sobriety of the significance of Iraq in recent events particularly helpful in its acknowledgement of the issue's complexities.' Janice emailed from Brisbane, Australia, saying, 'THANK YOU for speaking out today (on Radio National's "The World Today" – in Kirsten Aiken's report from London) about the killing of harmless people in Iraq. It's true it won't go away, and it is deep in our consciousness. But the media seems to have been biased towards the view that it's just. My husband has similar views to mine and is also grateful to you for speaking out. Congratulations on your walking achievement in spite of your vertigo. My ENT praised me for good management of my vertigo (I've had it for 3 years now).' And Paul from Youth Action for Peace UK wrote, 'Thank you for what you said. It seems ironic that the most level headed analysis of what is happening in our society should come from a victim of the London transport bombings – though no doubt being in that situation does concentrate the mind.'

Interestingly, Tim, a young publisher at Little, Brown, also heard the interview while getting up that morning. And he contacted me about writing this book.

SEVEN

Back to Being Academic

In the *Observer* on 24 July I caught sight again of the photo of Davinia Turrell being led away from Edgware Road Tube Station. I had first seen Davinia's image, wearing her surgical burns mask, in a huge full-page photograph on 8 July in the *Guardian* and in the *Independent,* where she was juxtaposed with a shot of me.

But this time, on 24 July, her picture was being used in a different context. It anchored a book review by Peter Preston, who in fact wrote a number of reviews that interested me over that two-month period when I couldn't read much. Even though I was off work and unable to write, I still had some academic tasks promised to other people – a book chapter on risk needed by colleagues at the University of Kent, and some research quality assessment to be done for the University of Ulster – and I was anxious to build up slowly towards being an academic again. I was still adopting Erin's and Maggie's strategy of setting small, strategic tasks, but although my colleagues at these other universities were being patient and supportive, they had their own deadlines and time would run out in due course.

In this way my strategy was, if I couldn't read (or write) academic books yet, maybe I could read book reviews, and Preston's review that day was of a new academic book in my field – *Mediated*, by the US scholar Thomas de Zengotita. I gave the review a try, and became fascinated.

According to Preston, de Zengotita was promoting a post-modern line about our world coming to us through a media prism, which colours our own self-definition – with all of us desperate to perform our part in that world of mediation, because that's all there is, nothing but images:

> Were the hundreds of thousands of mourners who turned out for Princess Di's funeral genuine mourners, gripped by genuine emotion? Perhaps, in a way: the mediated way of his title. But they were also volunteer players on an ad hoc stage, groundlings seeking their moment in history's arc light. And if that was true for Di, and for the thousands who thronged St Peter's Square when the Pope died on non-stop cable news, think what de Zengotita would have made of London two weeks ago and its silence for the slaughtered lambs.

I puzzled about the use of Davinia's image in its face mask to anchor this review. And I thought that Preston or his editor had chosen this one out of the full spectrum of 7/7 images because it was so theatrical. Masks have been associated with theatrical as well as real-life role-playing for centuries.

Looking at this just one day after I read of the killing of Jean Charles de Menezes, I wasn't in the mood for too much role-playing and cultural relativism. Death was death, and terrorism was terrorism. Still, I could see what Preston, via de Zengotita's book, was getting at:

> We are products of an immense, often inchoate, media indoc-trination. Moreover, the very pattern of life we take for

granted, our normality, is hectic, digital and new, quite different in kind from that of even recent generations. You know where you were when Kennedy or Di died or the Twin Towers came toppling down. But does anybody, except the few who were there, on the spot, remember Pearl Harbor? No, because no instant, vivid media existed to bring the enormity of that moment to you and make you share it. Our lives, as recently as the first half of the 20th century, were different in kind: isolated, unchanging, experiencing great events at a sluggardly distance.

Again, I thought (and I should emphasise quite how slow and laborious my reading process was then), what Preston was saying did make sense for the millions of people in London and round the world who were confronted by 7/7. That is how Janet in her flat in Camden Town first experienced the 'Attack on London', some hours before she got to see me, as an actual victim, with my face horribly scarred and swollen, in hospital that afternoon. But it was not how I had first experienced the terror, so I still wasn't satisfied. Then I read the review a bit further:

> If I am a sponge, an assemblage of images, sounds and influences, always looking out for my 15 minutes of fame, always rehearsing what I'll say if a camera pokes round my doorway or a producer from reality television comes knocking with a contract, then where is the real me, the inner core, not the outer show? ... On the morning of 9/11 de Zengotita was sitting in a park by Brooklyn Bridge. What was that bang? A gas main exploding? It's days before he's allowed to cross the East River to see for himself. 'It was chaos, a gigantic instantiation of necessity and accident'. It had cracked the expected frame of media representation. It was a tangle of shapes and miseries on a beautiful September day. It was – the exact word – surreal. More, much more than a Hollywood blockbuster: a

shattering experience because without the gloss of art or intellectual point or meaning, a glimpse of reality unmediated, the difference between watching a screen and being there amid dust and rubble.

By now, the review really was having an impact on me. On 7 July, in London, I had indeed found myself amid dust and rubble, less than three feet from a bomb that I didn't even hear. And ever since that time I had constantly been describing my experience of looking out of the rubble that morning at the other Tube train as surreal. Moreover, Preston's comments about 'always rehearsing what I'll say if a camera pokes round my doorway' fitted exactly my first perception of the image of Tony Blair at Gleneagles, supposedly first hearing about Davinia and me and all the other victims.

Yet I, too, had spent the two weeks since the explosion watching a screen – as a series of media images of myself on 7/7. Preston's review of *Mediated* was now making sense to me, especially when I thought about how I had been rebuilding my life via the media – 'watching a screen' – and my own memory of being there, which itself was constructed from a collection of discrete images in the rubble, and from conversations like that I had with Craig about his daughter's A-levels. It occurred to me now that my problem with the media in the past two weeks was not so much the issue of unethical practice – which the journalists who had invaded my ward on 8 July were accused of – but of how they were reconstructing my post-bomb experience even as it happened. Moreover, the media strategy that I was beginning to work out with Anton and Rowan was needed because I had found it difficult in the interviews I'd already had to get beyond my personal memories to the images of me that the media were producing. For me the main point was that most of the newspaper, TV and radio interviews I was giving seemed to edit out my thoughts on what the bomb that changed my life actually meant for me emotionally, economically, morally, politically, culturally and rhetorically. In the midst of a fake political consensus about Blair's so-called statesmanship, they were editing out my ideas on where the responsibilities lay.

Soon after reading Preston's review, I was asked by two Australian newspapers, the *Sydney Morning Herald* and the Melbourne *Age*, to write an 1100-word piece about my 7/7 experiences. With Anton and Rowan's considerable intellectual and stylistic help, I began to weave the Preston/de Zengotita idea into my very first writing assignment since the explosion. It was an important moment for me, because the review had engaged me intellectually and now I could feel active again, by writing about it and how I felt. Initially I put the Preston/de Zengotita stuff at the beginning of the article, to structure it. However, I was persuaded by Anton and Rowan to move it to the end so that the editors would feel the article started with impact, and was readable. They were right, because the *Sydney Morning Herald* edited out the academic stuff anyway. Nonetheless, it was a start for me, and about a month later I ordered de Zengotita's book from Amazon so that I could take his ideas further.

When I read *Mediated* itself, I enjoyed it enormously, because it is an extremely lively and convincing account of how life in Western societies in the twenty-first century is one of virtualities rather than realities, of how we live and self-consciously perform 'in a field of indefinitely many, always evolving options to be negotiated by reflexive individuals performing their lives according to improvised scripts they cobble together as they go along'.

This book is not the place to go far into *Mediated*, but if you read it I suspect you will be as enthralled as I was by the world of everyday examples de Zengotita clarifies with his theory: from teenagers' use of 'like' in every sentence to the practices of Blair and Bush. And he has counsel for me, too, about the use of my (and Davinia's) image in this world of virtualities, in the sense that I (or indeed, anyone else, including the media) only have a lease over my image:

> One may lease, as it were, a reading, but one never buys, for interpretations are bound to multiply, and no definitive documentation, no historical condition or authorial intent, will ever secure a settled meaning, and resolve the play of language – any more than the purpose of soap or shoes can restrain the way commodities are packaged and marketed as representations of something or other, or the way you construct yourself over time by choosing among these options – soap, shoes, health practices, readings, relationships, careers, whatever.

De Zengotita is masterly in his analysis of Bill Clinton and his performance (helped by intense media scrutiny) of the 'President's Penis', and he refers to Tony Blair as:

> The most exemplary of all Bill's progeny. Talk about legacy. Have you compared his shtick to the master's? You could swear he got hands-on lessons in expression and intonation management. But Blair just marks the trend. Leaders the world over are proceeding, more and more consciously, to turn themselves, their causes, their departments, universities, companies, parties, nations, and regions into well-positioned brand names. 'Traditional, but forward looking' was what some PR advisory committee to the Blair government called their vision statement for the New Britain. Says it all, doesn't it?

As for Bush, whom de Zengotita describes as a 'method actor . . . still a boy':

> You can feel him listening to himself, watching himself, rehearsing, practicing, just as he did all those years ago when

he first assumed the postures of Texas manliness – the arms held out from his body, fist side forward, swinging as he strides, and all the rest. That was how he decided to distinguish himself from patrician Easterners back home, people among whom he failed so utterly to be otherwise distinguished.

Take a look again at Bush walking with Blair through the assembled heads of state at Gleneagles in TV footage of the morning of 7 July 2005 and you will see what de Zengotita means. But his point is that we all in the West – the patrician Easterners, the young man who helped Davinia to safety, you as you read and me as I write – are playing this game of virtualities and image-making.

And yet this is not in fact de Zengotita's whole world. There is a dark shadow lurking behind his cool, convincing and feisty postmodern book. He first raises the shadow in his preface:

> Most important, this acknowledgement: millions of human beings are trapped in realities so restrictive, so desperate, that the possibility of applying to them what I have to say in this book does not arise at all. But the issue of the real trend remains, for it is global. And so does the issue of mediated reality in relation to the immiseration of those millions, not as it is lived, but as it is experienced by the rest of us, by privileged citizens of the overdeveloped world who can choose to deal with it. Or not.

He returns to this theme in the very last words of the book, at the end of his chapter 'Coda: Terror': 'The bubble of self-regarding self-representation that has insulated us for so long from the suffering of millions in a world dominated by our interests and institutions – that bubble will reform around us, and cradle us again. Until the next time.' By 'the next time' de

Zengotita means the next terror strike – because the condition he describes as surreal is that one of forced contrast between our manufactured world of self-regarding images and the actual sight, smell, 'flesh and stone of events' at Ground Zero:

> The surreality of everyday life in a bubble of privilege pierced by terror [after the 9/11 attack] was nourished in the early days by a mood very like angst, but not quite, because this possibility was real. The object of this mood was miasmic, lurking in the mail, the water, the food, the air. The very ground was suspended in possibility. The mighty bridges, the highways and tunnels, the mountainous buildings – all the landmarks, as they are so aptly called, those orienting monuments [the Twin Towers] that were once as settled as north or south or up and down; their necessity was drained away. Once apparent only to artists and metaphysicians, the contingency of all things became apparent to everyone. It was as if the world were saturated with some new colour.

For me the colour of the surreal was yellow as my orienting monument, the Tube train carriage, was stretched and disassembled, and I encountered what de Zengotita describes as the contingency of 'chaos, a gigantic instantiation of necessity and accident. Suddenly, your point of view had no special claim.'

But, as de Zengotita says, politicians will continue to perform – 'must be seen to act' – even at these times of the 'absence of representation'. He speaks savagely of politicians and 9/11:

> And the official atmosphere, the effect of the performances of those others, the famous ones in government and media? They contributed their dollop to the mood, in the beginning, by way of inadequacies they could not hide, moments when they verged on hysteria, others in which they seemed bent on

self-parody . . . They helped to sustain the suspension of our world in existential possibility by saying the only thing that could truly be said in the first few weeks and months, namely, 'Go back to normal, but be alert, because death could strike at any moment'. People anxious to believe in a semblance of normality got very annoyed at the authorities for saying this. After all, they had come to rely upon them for every sort of assistance in creating and sustaining facades and rationaliza- tions, for stories that help them feel good about themselves. Suddenly (for self-interested reasons, but never mind), these same authorities were communicating a profound truth . . . And so those in charge, abandoning the profundity they had touched upon, took up the stern-but-loving parent role, one of their favourites, and proceeded to lecture us about 'A dif- ferent world now . . . Londoners during the blitz'.

De Zengotita wrote that about 9/11 before 7/7 happened, but every word rings true again for the events of July and their aftermath, for me anyway. This Blitz mentality – and the sub- sequent media focus on the causality of terror among 'hate preachers' and 'asylum rejects' – is part of what de Zengotita calls 'the virtualizing effect of coverage' which:

> will work as a natural antidote to the surrealizing effect of the possibility of terror, but for as long as that possibility is real, it will not entirely succeed . . . The possibility of mass terror haunts the world. It's a different order of reality. And, no matter how exhaustively the agents of mediation cover terror, they cannot 'cover' its possibility. They can represent what hap- pened after it happens, they can represent what might happen in this or that case – that is, they can depict specific possibilities endlessly – but they can't depict the sheer possibility they nev- ertheless evoke . . . That's part of the unrepresentable mood that eludes mediation at the dawn of the age of terror.

What de Zengotita is describing is not so much culture clash or the clash of civilisations but a profound tension between our Western world of postmodern virtuality, in which the possibilities of choice and self-aware performance seem endless, and the world of millions of others who are 'dominated by our interests'. Nonetheless, as he says at the end of his chapter on identity politics, so much of Bush's (and Blair's) 'facades have been shredded, and the age of terror posits a reality that media cannot cover'.

More academic thinking: new wars theory

Thomas de Zengotita's stories in *Mediated* were leading me back to my academic identity as surely as Craig Staniforth's stories brought me back to my bodily one. With that intellectual hunger re-established, I could look back to other areas of work I had recently been immersed in, which might help explain how the suffering of so many is positioned rhetorically by our leaders.

In January 2005 I had given a keynote paper at a conference on risk at the University of Canterbury, where I had spoken about images in the media in the context of contemporary warfare. I made reference to theorists like Mary Kaldor, Mark Duffield, Michael Humphrey and Allen Feldman, and the concept of 'new wars'. Overall, these theorists thoroughly reject the Bush/Blair idea that the world has changed for ever post-9/11 and 7/7. Rather, they argue that the political rhetoric about wars like Iraq and the 'war against terror' is contiguous with earlier military interventions such as that in Kosovo. At that time, a new political lexicon for describing intra-state or non-state violence and warfare came into being to justify new wars. So terms like 'ethnic cleansing', 'genocide' and 'terrorism' began to be used to validate new military interventions, rationalised variously in the media and by politicians either as a 'humanitarian war', 'militaristic humanism', a 'war against terror' or most recently (in the case of Iraq) as a 'pre-emptive war'.

These new wars were often framed to remove states' leaders who aimed to injure and kill entire populations, or traumatise them into submission or flight – precisely the Western media discourse surrounding the 1999 Kosovo war against Slobodan Milosevic and the 2003 Iraq war against Saddam Hussein. Blair's resort to calling the Iraq war a humanitarian cause was so seamless and easy – after the lies about weapons of mass destruction had been exposed (coded, 'intelligence inadequacies') – because the notion of getting rid of monstrously bad guys like Saddam or Milosevic was already common currency, already in public discourse.

However, Mary Kaldor has argued that rather than being explained by specific good guy/bad guy causes like ethnic conflict, these new wars are in fact marked by the erosion of state monopoly over legitimate violence. This has come from above, in the creation of war networks – the coming together of militaries, UN agencies, donor governments, non-governmental organisations and the corporate sector, such as happened in the Iraq war. It has also come from below, and can be seen in the 'privatisation' of violence by paramilitary groups, breakaway groups from regular armies, local warlords, insurgency groups, mercenaries, criminal gangs – and terrorists. New wars theorists have thus come to see terrorism as an extension of privatised violence in a post-Cold War world where politicians' new talk is about 'periphery states', 'failed states' and 'rogue states'.

According to Mark Duffield, networks of intervention and dependence are established very early – before new wars actually begin – between militaries, major international institutions, like the UN, the Organisation for Security and Co-operation in Europe, the Organisation for Economic Co-operation and

Development, the World Bank and NGO and donor organisations. The aim of these alliances is not specifically the recovery of national sovereignty in failed states, but rather a new global interventionism on behalf of democratisation, stability through reconstruction and the free market – precisely the scenario in Iraq, as well as the agenda of the G8 Summit at Gleneagles.

Duffield argues that this idea of security and development, with its project of liberal peace, constructs the world's poor as victims, denying them the right to express their grievances by way of violence, while vilifying and criminalising the leaders of violence. In a series of case studies, he has described the networks of local warlords, militaries, aid agencies, financial institutions and multinational corporations that enable the new wars. Michael Humphrey notes the further parallel between the media relations of new wars and 'liberal peace', drawing on Allen Feldman to argue that 'mediatized images of danger and risk are circulated as "risk events" open to manipulation by both state and terrorists. The spectatorship of events is central to the public safety wars as well as to the terrorist challenge to the legitimacy of war making and peace making'.

The point that these academics are making in their rather complex arguments is that all of us, through various manipulation and mobilisation of the media – by political leaders and by terrorists alike – have become fearful spectators of a constant succession of 'risk events'. Feldman notes the regular circulation of these by the media, as we confront, in rapid succession, AIDS, BSE, SARS, avian flu, terrorism and no doubt a host of things yet unknown. So, these new wars, Feldman argues, function as 'cultural imaginaries' – of popular fear and surveillance – rather than solely as military or geo-strategic instruments. This explains just why immigration and asylum become such potent targets for the media. Borders – against avian flu, SARS or terrorism – become harder to control in de Zengotita's world of virtualisation.

But equally, as Michael Humphrey emphasises, what we see of warfare is controlled not only by powerful politicians like Blair and media magnates like Rupert Murdoch. The networked association of al-Qaeda, al-Jazeera and American and British TV brought Osama bin Laden directly before US voters just prior to the November 2004 presidential election. It also brought the video of Mohammad Sidique Khan to the British public soon after 7/7. Much of the anger and outrage expressed by politicians and media at these pictures of terrorists in our midst came from their realising how permeable our borders actually are. The image of Mohammad Sidique Khan in his terrorist's regalia was made so much more uncomfortable for British people, as we heard constantly through the media, by the fact that he spoke with a Yorkshire accent and blamed us for re-electing Blair after the Iraq fiasco.

The struggle between mainstream media and these frighteningly subversive terrorist media images is a constant of our experience as fearful spectators. Kirsty Best talks, for example, about the stark contrast between the images from Iraq we were receiving early in the war, when the use of embedded journalism and 'Shock and Awe' rhetoric disguised the degree of civilian horror, and the graphic images quickly provided by al-Jazeera of both Iraqi and American casualties (much to Donald Rumsfeld's fury). Then, in addition to al-Jazeera's transmissions, the images of Abu Ghraib, themselves taken by US soldiers using digital cameras, created, Best argues, a problematic excess for governments, and allowed viewers worldwide to 'readily relate to the pain, suffering and confusion permeating the images of a tortured body'.

I can't begin to describe how this mixture of images affected me in the weeks and months after I was injured so badly by Mohammad Sidique Khan. Certainly these academic theories were making a lot of sense to me, about the Gleneagles 'Make Poverty History' rhetoric, about the contrast of surreal and performative images that impacted on me from the time the bomb went off and about the contrast between images of the suicide bomber in my carriage in British newspapers and those on al-Jazeera. But I also knew that I wanted to go beyond the polarity that Kirsty Best describes of 'official' and 'other' media to the words and voices of other people who were asking questions. It was in those months after July, when I began to regain a bit of mobility, that I started to look at what other British people – in the theatre, in literature, on radio, on TV and the press and even in reviewing art exhibitions – were now asking about Iraq and 7/7.

EIGHT

Replacing the Culture of Fear

In August 2005, for the first time since the attacks, I ventured into crowded public places again. I had no idea how I would fare at packed football grounds, huge theatres and concerts, or even in small cinemas – entertainments that were very much part of my life with family and friends before the bombings. I probably wouldn't have tried to find out as early as August, but I had long ago booked tickets for that month at Chichester Festival Theatre.

I had bought the tickets as part of my old life researching theatre audiences. I had recently published an academic book in that area, and after that had begun to focus more closely on a spate of plays in 2004 and 2005 referencing the Iraq war and the 'war against terror', most with some critical acclaim.

I guessed I was going to feel different compared with my theatre visits of a year earlier, but I didn't know how being a bomb victim would affect me as an academic, intellectually and emotionally. I'm going to try to write about that in this chapter, even though I'm still far from clear about it all. I didn't even begin to get my thoughts on this together until October and November

2005, by which time I had been reading more newspaper articles.

Among these on 1 October I found the following comment from Joanna Bourke in the *Guardian*: 'The great paradox of this new form of warfare is that our survival depends as much upon our response to our own political leaders as our response to the terrorists themselves.' After reading this and a quote from Nicholas Kent, the artistic director of the Tricycle Theatre in north London ('I've never lost the sense that theatre is here to empower us, to give us a voice in the democratic process. Politicians are doing the opposite.'), I began to think about my responses at the Chichester performances. Four public events – the terrorist attacks of 7 July, the performance of a play about an earlier British terrorist attack, the ejection from a Labour Party conference of one of its members on the basis of anti-terror legislation and the award of the Nobel Prize for Literature to a British playwright who spoke publicly about the 'war against terror' – are central to this chapter, too. My focus is to examine the public voices on behalf of democratic civil engagement that have insistently offered an alternative to the spin of politicians on new kinds of warfare and the 'war against terror'.

The public voices may be those of academics speaking more widely than just in their lecture halls, like Joanna Bourke writing in the *Guardian*:

> In the new conflicts of the 21st century – conducted by global terrorists, who possess contradictory and unrealistic goals – a new paradigm of resistance is needed ... Strengthening democratic liberties and replacing a culture of fear with one of ethical responsibility and civic engagement are the only viable long-term responses to terrorism.

They may be those of theatre directors like Nicholas Kent, or of playwrights like Harold Pinter, quoted on the front page of the *Independent* the day after he was awarded the Nobel Prize:

> A formidable assertion of military force [has been] responsible for the deaths and mutilation of thousands upon thousands of innocent people ... [N]either the US nor the UK bother to count the Iraqi dead . . . We have brought torture, cluster bombs, innumerable acts of random murder, misery and degradation to the Iraqi people and call it 'bringing freedom and democracy to the Middle East'. But, as we all know, we have not been welcomed with the predicted flowers. What we have unleashed is a ferocious and unwitting resistance, mayhem and chaos.

The voices may come from television or newspaper professionals. They may be those of political party activists, or of famous novelists. But whatever public channel of communication they adopt, they are all important, vocal parts of a groundswell of alternative political voices in the UK. They all engage directly with a British and an international culture of fear. They all, in Joanna Bourke's words, are asking questions about an alternative democracy of ethical responsibility and civic engagement.

The Iraq plays

I believe the voices of the theatre are symptomatic – both in their open, dialogic form and in their critical content – of a much wider feeling among British public intellectuals. British theatre, through 2004 and 2005, has consistently and critically explored the issues thrown up by the war in Iraq. The *Guardian* theatre reviewer Michael Billington noted as early as June 2004 that there was a spreading rash of Greek tragedies in Britain which were being interpreted in the light of Iraq and the 'war against terror'. At that time, I was interested to see whether this kind of theatre would touch a nerve among close friends and colleagues, who I knew felt keenly a sense of having been disempowered politically over the war. I wondered whether people who felt like this were enjoying these plays, and what they were getting out of them.

I had already done research for about twenty-five years on TV audiences, and (like most of my cultural studies colleagues) had become interested in the differences in audience response, depending on age, gender, sexual preference, class, ethnicity and so on. In recent years I had begun to focus on the relationship in live theatre between audience and performer, in contrast to the mediated experience of TV viewers. At the same time, as a researcher on the theory of risk, I had also been tracing the coverage in British newspapers of contemporary warfare, from Kosovo to Iraq. In July 2004, exactly a year before the terrorist attacks, I put together these two academic interests by researching the audiences for a Greek tragedy-derived play about terrorism, *Cruel and Tender*, at Chichester.

Cruel and Tender

Cruel and Tender is based on Sophocles' *Trachiniae (Women of Trachis)*. Deianeira (Amelia in *Cruel and Tender*) awaits the return of Hercules (the General in *Cruel and Tender*) who has been away fighting a brutal war. He sends home his female captives, one of whom is his concubine. Deianeira tries to win him back with a love potion rubbed on to a tunic (a nerve agent inserted into a pillow in *Cruel and Tender*), but it kills him. She then kills herself in her bed.

I chose this play because many critics in British newspapers saw it as part of a wider theatrical event. In the middle of 2004, against the backdrop of the 'war against terror', a sequence of

Greek tragedies were performed in the UK, and they tended to be reviewed together. Georgina Brown in the *Mail on Sunday* on 27 June 2004 said:

> Theatre was at war this week, in a direct and searching response to the Iraq invasion. Fascinatingly, it's to the ancient Greeks that director Katie Mitchell has turned for amplification, with a new version of Euripides' tragedy *Iphigenia at Aulis* . . . Tony Blair and George Bush are not killing their own children to win a war but they are, by default, killing other people's children . . . This brilliantly performed piece brings into sharp focus the notion of political expediency, of doing the wrong thing for the right reasons.
>
> *Cruel and Tender*, Martin Crimp's version of a play by Sophocles, is also a world away from being all Greek and mythical. Crimp not only brings it bang up-to-date but makes it extraordinarily topical. Try hearing the words, 'If you want to root out terror there is only one rule – kill' without thinking of Iraq and all the attempts we've heard from politicians to justify the invasion of Iraq, before it and subsequently . . . [Director] Bondy, like Crimp, is at pains to suggest . . . that the war on terror creates more terror . . .
>
> *Guantanamo* cuts to the quick in a series of statements from a handful of the 650 people, several of whom are British Asians, held in prison camps, often in chains, in cages or in solitary confinement, in Cuba and here in Britain. Their crime? To be Muslims, and therefore suspected terrorists . . . This shocking, harrowing account, all the more potent for the stoicism and lack of sensationalism with which it is delivered, should not just be seen but acted upon.

Similarly, at the other end of the political spectrum, on 19 June Michael Billington in the *Guardian* reviewed together *Iphigenia at Aulis*, *Cruel and Tender* and *Hecuba*:

What these revivals all have in common is that they are a direct response to the Iraq war . . . Katie Mitchell, who directs *Iphigenia at Aulis* at the National, said: 'I was looking for a play that could have a conversation with the audience about what was happening in Iraq. This is a play that takes a cynical and satirical look at the actions of public figures . . . unlike Euripides' Agamemnon, who sacrifices his daughter, Tony Blair is not actually killing his own children. But what we recognise in this and other Greek plays is the gap between politicians who talk in moral absolutes and our own sense that everything is muddy, complex and confused.'

What is striking is that everyone involved in the current Greek revivals sees the plays as topical works rather than cultural artefacts. Martin Crimp's *Cruel and Tender*, adapted from Sophocles' *Trachiniae*, is set in a world where cities are pulverized, liberators turn aggressors and violence is expediently justified . . . The director, Luc Bondy, said 'I came across Sophocles' play . . . and found in it something that resonated with a world seeking to justify the invasion of Iraq . . . Sophocles used a myth the audience all knew to comment on his own time. In a similar way we are using Sophocles' play as a way of illuminating ours.'

Jonathan Kent, who directs the Donmar production [of *Hecuba*] opening in September, sees it as more than a study of individual desperation . . . It would be a great mistake to see the action explicitly outside Basra or Baghdad. Yet it would also be a sign of failure if the play didn't bring Iraq to mind.

The Iraq war may not be the only reason why Greek plays are popular . . . But in the end it is the Greek understanding of the human consequences of war and of the gulf between public rhetoric and private feeling that makes these plays seem shockingly relevant to our own divided world.

It was clear from my initial research that these plays were being seen as a significant event by reviewers across the political spectrum. But what kind of event was it? Newspaper reviews continued to focus on their shocking relevance to our own leaders' killing of innocent people abroad (as Pinter also emphasised). They did not miss, either, the parallel with how political rhetoric was used to try to manage public feeling. There was also plenty of speculation as to why so many Greek tragedies were being produced. As Michael Billington wrote, 'Where does our theatre instinctively turn in times of crisis? Not to Shakespeare or Shaw but to the Greeks.' Edith Hall wrote in the programme notes for Tony Harrison's *Hecuba* that 'the play dramatises the total failure of those social institutions, such as arenas for political debate and law, that are supposed to regulate the expression of human passions and prevent injustice and atrocity'.

So Harold Pinter's political position over his November 2005 Nobel Prize award where he excoriated a half-century of US foreign policy was already being prepared for by a groundswell of British theatre as early as mid-2004. Among newspaper critics – as with Pinter – there was a strong sense that theatre could provide a political outlet for public feeling. These were productions, Georgina Brown said, which should not only be seen but acted upon. Theatre was becoming an alternative forum for debate in an otherwise diminished democratic public sphere.

This feeling was especially strong around the time of the production of *Cruel and Tender*, due mainly to the very recent and massive media coverage of Abu Ghraib. The shocking photographs all newspapers carried from the US prison camp in Iraq would almost certainly have been in the minds of people who went to these plays. They were definitely in the minds of theatre reviewers. In the *Daily Telegraph* on 15 May, Charles Spencer wrote:

Nothing I have seen in the theatre to date so resonantly and provocatively captures our bewildering post-9/11 world, with its alarmingly amorphous war against terrorism and the ghastly aftershocks coming out of Iraq . . . Just a week ago, I might have thought Crimp was being hysterical in his account of a Western soldier supposedly fighting terror but actually succumbing to the same vile tactics as his enemy. The dreadful pictures from the Abu Ghraib jail have undermined that comfortably complacent view and Crimp's play powerfully demonstrates the insidiously infectious nature of evil . . . [and] seems to bring us close to the heart of contemporary darkness.

Similarly, on 14 May, Nicholas de Jongh wrote in the *Evening Standard*:

[*Cruel and Tender*] which takes its plot and characters from Sophocles' *Women of Trachis*, is not exactly distant from our own world of terrorism and Anglo-American soldiery accused of war crimes . . . The ancient Greek world and our own come to seem magically conjoined in the nemesis of the General's last exit.

British theatre reviewers of all political affiliations were moved by the powerful synergy between the horror over recent events in Iraq, the dismay at politicians' spin and the highly visceral performances on stage. On 8 April 2005 Michael Billington wrote of the production of *Hecuba* at the Albery Theatre:

Right from the off, [Tony] Harrison insinuatingly suggests the play's modernity. The ghost of Polydorus says that Priam, his father, feared Troy would 'end up occupied by the Greek coalition'. And that smooth apologist for barbarism, Odysseus, in reminding Hecuba her daughter, Polyxena, is to be sacrificed, says: 'I'll spin through it again so that we're all

clear'. No-one comes on crudely dressed as Bush or
Rumsfeld. But Harrison never lets us forget the aching
topicality of Euripides' study of the powerful and the powerless. At one point the singing chorus of Trojan women
recall the sacking of their city by the slaughter-gutted, sex-
starved Greek troops who cried 'let's finish it off and fuck off
home'. Even the four-letter word earns its place by jolting us
into awareness of the modern parallels.

It does indeed, as anyone who has read recent autobiogra-
phies by US soldiers in Iraq will know. However, because it is
live, theatre has a major advantage over books or other mass
media in bringing horror right into our faces. It is embodied in
actual men and women performing a few metres from where we
sit. Like Billington, Paul Taylor in the *Independent*, on 24 May,
put his emphasis on the lethally visceral nature of *Cruel and
Tender*:

> Half-naked, his penis in a catheter, his skin hideously blighted
> by the chemical weapons equivalent of the hessian shirt, Joe
> Dixon's wheel-chaired General derangedly insists that he has
> 'burnt terror' out of the world for the people . . . There's a
> sequence that viscerally involves you to a truly tension-induc-
> ing degree when, realising what she has done, half-drunk and
> with a crushed wineglass in her hand, Amelia [Kerry Fox]
> staggers bleeding round the compound to a counterpoint of
> a piercingly pure German oratorio. Already, around her, the
> furniture is being covered in the polythene sheets and the
> room turned into the 'crime scene' it will become after she is
> dead.

I can confirm personally, having seen the production of
Cruel and Tender at both London's Young Vic and the
Chichester Festival Theatre, that this was indeed a highly

visceral production, with Joe Dixon's near-naked General the most muscular performance of crazed masculinity and militarism I have ever seen. From audience responses I heard myself at both theatres, it was clear there was real emotional shock at these particular scenes played by Kerry Fox (the crushed wineglass in her bleeding hand) and Joe Dixon (hurling his urine bag at attendants).

The link between the physical performances on stage and images we had all seen from recent warfare was clear to *Cruel and Tender*'s writer, Martin Crimp. He himself had responded from the start to images of male military madness and female pain: 'As for the background of terror, political hypocrisy, and a city destroyed for a lie, I didn't have to look very far to discover a congruent universe.' It was from the universe of the new warfare that Crimp took some very powerful images into his writing of the play:

> I began by collecting photographs. In one, a Liberian commander – a boy of about 20 – leaps into the air with an enormous smile to camera as if he's just scored a goal, rather than fired a rocket-propelled grenade. In the foreground, next to the spent cartridges, a blue flip-flop.
>
> In another, an American soldier 'carries an Iraqi child from a house in a dawn raid'. The soldier, whose eyes are lowered in concentration and who seems – oddly – to be wearing rimless glasses, has one arm round a small, crying boy. At the centre of the black doorway, and of the photograph, is the soldier's red glove.
>
> In a third a woman runs along a Sarajevo pavement – from what? Sniper fire? Mortar rounds? – while a UN soldier takes aim with his rifle at some threat out of the frame. The woman's clothes are tight to her skin: even her hair is up, exposing her skin; conversely, the man's body is covered and distorted by the armour of war.

Crimp was clearly moved and motivated by the almost surreal contrasts in these images: the everyday blue flip-flop and
the red glove next to scenes of rampant male militarism; and
the woman, tightly clothed and her skin exposed, juxtaposed
with the robotically alien soldier.

One explanation for the number of Greek tragedies being
produced can be found in the powerful gender roles they
explored. Crimp talks about the idea of 'feminising' the enemy
via anal rape as happened in both the 1991 Gulf War and 425
BC Peloponnesian War. And academic Edith Hall writes in the
2004 Chichester Festival programme of four decades of femi-
nist influence on Greek tragedy revivals in Britain.

Nonetheless, the strength of the gender performances in
Cruel and Tender that Luc Bondy emphasised – 'neither the wife
nor the mistress are victims' – is only part of the public appeal
of this play. As live performance, again and again reviewers
and audiences were attracted and moved by what Charles
Spencer in the *Daily Telegraph* called 'muscular' and 'anguished'
moments onstage which make 'the stomach knot with tension
and terror'.

Much better than hearing yet more self-serving politicians'
rhetoric about Iraq or terrorism, British theatre audiences
have been confronted with alternative ethical dilemmas in
such physically shocking ways, focusing less on individual
character than on what critic Sarah Hemmings called 'fluctuations and constellations' in relationships. Across two
performances of *Cruel and Tender* at two different theatres, what
I most remembered was an extraordinarily volatile and gut-
wrenching set of warring human 'fluctuations': Amelia's son
with his pillow hard over her face, after she has used him
hideously and fatally to harm his father; and the slightly built
son sitting on his hugely muscular father's wheelchaired knee
in the last Act – after Amelia is seen bleeding and dead – as
the two men work through their own generational, physical

and political differences. In each case – the son threatening to kill his mother, the father emasculating his son – a sense of terrorism ready, growing and willing in all of us, is absolute. This is what Martin Crimp means when he talks of Sophocles' Hydra analogy, since the play fluctuates as each character in turn – the mother, the son and the father – becomes a terrorist to the other:

> Heracles – or Hercules – was the archetypal warrior-hero and original destroyer of terror. What else is this Hydra – the multi-headed snake which, for every head Heracles severed, grew two in its place – but a stranger foreshadowing terrorism? ... In Sophocles' *Trachiniae* the warrior hero, unable to stop killing, razes an entire city to abduct the girl he's obsessed with and sends her home to his own wife, whose attempt to win back his love results only in the violent death of the protagonists. That is the play I have rewritten as *Cruel and Tender*.

The analogy between the Hydra and terrorism is not just the simple one that for every insurgent killed in Iraq two grow in his place. It also points – via Amelia's deathly relationship with her husband's mistress – to the proliferation of terror within our home base, within our own country and even within our own families.

The greater power of the writing is in this many-headed Hydra sense, that each woman oppressed, each son oppressed, each racially different person oppressed and each servant or slave oppressed is the potential source of more killing, control, oppression, terrorism and tragedy.

Hecuba, played in two major productions in London in 2004, contained another classic version of Crimp's survivor-as-terrorist, as the Trojan War-humiliated and betrayed queen extends her horror over the killing of her children by cutting into pieces – into a see-through bag of body parts – the young children of one of her oppressors. But Edith Hall's conclusion to her piece 'What have the Greeks to say to the Third Millennium?' reminded me that there may now be another kind of survivor-as-terrorist:

> The term 'survivor' is one of the hallmarks of our age. It was originally just a legal term denoting relatives of a deceased person who were to be beneficiaries of a will . . . But the term now covers those who have suffered from disease, addiction, and especially damage knowingly inflicted by and on people. Incest survivors, rape survivors, concentration camp survivors, genocide survivors, Holocaust survivors, Hiroshima survivors – our new tragic heroes are those who have learned somehow to accommodate unbearable memories of acute trauma, including trauma for which they themselves are responsible, and live with their psychological pain.

As Hall says, the bad guys in Shakespearean and Jacobean tragedy strewed the stage at the end with their dead bodies, but in Greek tragedy the 'heroes are true survivors in the most modern sense of the term':

> The incestuous Oedipus, the infanticidal Hercules, Medea, and Agave, the mother-murdering Orestes, the bereaved women of Troy, Heracles' traumatised son – they all survive their terrible experiences and stagger from the stage leaving the audience wondering how they can possibly cope with their psychological burdens. It is perhaps in this respect more than in any other that Greek tragedy has chimed with the obsessions of an age which has itself only just survived the man-made horrors of the twentieth century.

Chiming with our experience of the new warfare, Hall is suggesting, we, too, have to go on living with our guilt. Not all survivors kill in chain reaction, like Hecuba. The point is that the survivor – like me in my hospital bed at St Mary's – can also be an implicit, maybe unwilling terrorist in Martin Crimp's sense – in so far as Blair did fight the state-terrorist war over Iraq in my name. And Blair fought the war in part against those Fallujah victims whom I began to empathise with in hospital, even as I clung to the medical care that they were denied. I can recall those feelings and also, at that time, seeing the photograph of Blair, his head down, receiving the news of the bombings. And it was then that I remembered Martin Crimp's words:

> Of course, the writers of fifth-century Athens didn't need to collect cuttings to understand wars, they experienced them . . . So when I re-examine these photos – young commander leaping, soldier both rescuing and terrorising child, woman running from gunfire – I'm aware of my own privileged distance from death and dismemberment. No one (currently) is raiding my house . . .
>
>   These pictures are windows, yes, on to events, but at the same time – let's be frank about this – reflections of our own anxiety. The darker it gets outside, the blacker a window becomes, and the more it turns into a mirror.

The difference, it seems, between these playwrights, directors and performers on the one hand and Blair on the other, is that he doesn't see his own image reflected in the blackening window.

But what did the actual audiences at Chichester think about *Cruel and Tender*? One question in the survey of the play's audiences asked if they agreed or disagreed with a quote about it by *Observer* reviewer Susannah Clapp: 'The war in Iraq has made Greek tragedy essential . . . [I]t's really the prevailing sense of powerlessness that's the conclusive link between then and now.'

Over 50 per cent of returned questionnaires did agree directly with Clapp's view, revealing that audience members felt disempowered both personally and politically. There was also a significant reference to feeling guilt, as in this kind of response to Clapp's comment about powerlessness: 'If you mean that we are all guilty and/or contaminated to a degree, then, yes, I do [agree].' Another audience member speaks of feeling complete 'public powerlessness – the future is becoming dictatorial. Blair does not respond to other than his own internal forces and post-PM USA lecture tours. Nothing matters apart from Bush winning the next election. Stuff happens'. And another talks of much greater need for cultural recognition:

> Yes, I am against the war in Iraq as I have spent many years living in M. East, have many Arab/Muslim friends. I do not think Bush knows about M. East way of life, tribal associations, religious tolerance to Christians, etc except in Saudi Arabia.

It seems that Susannah Clapp and I were far from being alone in our responses to *Cruel and Tender*. Some felt it asked questions, rather than gave answers, and many saw the play as about feelings of disempowerment:

> Yes, it [is], which is a shame as individually we can all be empowered in our own lives to effect change.

> Yes, I agree, our inability to act in the face of terror . . . And the frustration of being unable to influence or change events, especially evil ones perpetrated in one's own name.

> Is there a prevailing sense of public powerlessness? The play points to the possibility, rather than promotes the idea. Makes people think, not propaganda.

5/11

In August 2005, just a month after the explosion at Edgware Road, I was back at the Chichester Festival Theatre. It was not, though, as the academic researcher I had been just one year before, armed, as I was then, with tape recorder, questionnaires and focus group methodology. The very feel of the theatre was different for me now. Everything I had done this August – bathing, walking outside, being taken by ambulance to hospital, making my first uncertain visits to a cinema and then to a theatre, taking my first taxi, Tube and train trips – had to be done with carers, family or friends. My professional carers, Maggie and Erin, had gone painstakingly through every stage with me: how to duck and weave when I first walked through the streets of Camden Town; how to try to avoid nausea by my choice of train and seating to Brighton; and, now, how to prepare for my visit to the theatre in Chichester.

We agreed that the first thing I'd do when I got there was talk to people at the box office about my problem, and look at seating plans with them. If possible I would change my seat to one near an exit, in case I got nauseous or was traumatised by the performance. There was a new connection for me with this particular play: *5/11* was a contemporary take on the terrorism of the 1605 Gunpowder Plot. In fact, when I got to Chichester, sympathetic staff warned me straight away that all three plays I was seeing – the other two were Phyllis Nagy's rewriting of Nathaniel Hawthorne's novel *The Scarlet Letter*, and Molière's *Scapino or the Trickster* – had lots of light flashes and explosions. Moreover, they told me that the seat I had for my first showing, at the more intimate Minerva Theatre for *The Scarlet Letter*, which on the plan seemed close to an exit, was in fact several feet above it and cut off from escape by a barrier.

So my first contact with each of the plays I now saw was physical in a very personal way. Where was I sitting? How could

I escape if I needed to vomit during the performance? Would I even manage to go into *5/11* given that the performance was sold out and my prebooked seat was near the middle of a row close to the stage in the main Festival Theatre? Marian, like Anton and Rowan before, had arrived from Australia and been reconfigured by Maggie and Erin's strategies to act as a helper. This was essential to me because I didn't know whether I would feel okay to go into the theatre until shortly before the bell sounded. Even after I'd got to my seat, I still felt tense and this all needed to be managed.

Just before the performance of *5/11* something else caught my attention. I had wondered why I didn't feel guilty enjoying plays in Chichester just a month after fifty-two people had died in terrorist attacks around me, and my eye was caught by Phyllis Nagy's response in *The Scarlet Letter* programme to a question about audiences and guilt:

> I think that people find it very easy to make guilt an abstraction in their daily lives – to look at a Rwandan appeal, or to personalise it even further, a friend dying of AIDS, and to just sort of go through the motions of guilt, and give a little money, or go to a memorial service and that's an end of it. I think we might be a little healthier if from time to time we did experience that personal and profound fusion of guilt and self-inflicted torture. It might be quite constructive!

Standing in the sunshine outside the Festival Theatre among the wine-drinkers and the picnickers, I thought right then that even if my torture hadn't exactly been self-inflicted (I hadn't even voted for Blair!), I had been through a great deal of guilt and pain in my hospital bed. So how constructive might that be in seeing this play about terrorism?

At first the flashes and the crowds, and a considerable frustration at Hugh Ross (playing Cecil) not projecting his voice as loudly as the others (my hearing was still much reduced), pre-occupied me. However, the theme of the festival quickly began to work through the thoughts and feelings I'd been having since the attacks. It was all about 'con art', covering tricksters, government spin, sexually and politically deviant performances, and outsiders whose in-your-face actions exposed the whole political and moral edifice of their place and time. An eighty-two-year-old man at the New Labour Party conference, and a seventy-five-year-old playwright awarded a Nobel Prize, were about to do just that, too. But at the time, as I watched Phyllis Nagy's *The Scarlet Letter*, Edward Kemp's *5/11* and Jeremy Sam's translation of Molière's *Scapino*, I found myself thinking about the festival's questions about tricksters.

In his programme notes for *Scapino*, Edward Kemp expanded on the theme (which also included Gogol's *The Government Inspector*) by drawing attention to the close relationship between acting, politics and our everyday lives. First, there is the performance of acting. Kemp finds this in *Scapino*, which promotes the actor's pleasure in verbal and visual disguise, yet ends in the Chichester production with the leading character's despair over the 'falsity and duplicity of the world that surrounds him'. Second, the same scenario could easily have been conceived in the performance of politics by Gogol's *The Government Inspector* – as Kemp says, Gogol's Russia had endless con artists among its bureaucrats and government functionaries. But what the production pointed to was a third area of con artistry – the performance as con artists of all of us: 'The "con" [the government inspector] perpetrates on the nameless town . . . is actually executed by the inhabitants themselves. What Gogol brilliantly shows is that in a culture where spin and trickery have become so prevalent, nobody can any longer recognise the innocent truth staring them in the face.' It is not hard to find in Kemp's eyeballing of the festival theme, a close analogy with the mix of government con artists, spin and manipulation of the media and a contemporary British public's supposedly innocent participation in it all.

The focus of the festival was always, of course, each play itself emerging out of its own highly collective process of rehearsal – what Luc Bondy called the inventive 'space to find out how people are, how they behave together'. Nevertheless, the Chichester festival theme did encourage audiences, via programme pieces like Kemp's, to make connections themselves about how the plays behave together. This was helped by the overall sense that this is a festival, because a significant proportion of the audiences stay in Chichester for two or three days, picnicking between plays on the lawns and having more time to read programme notes and chat with each other about them than playgoers usually do.

There would certainly have been a lot more people than just me reading Kemp's programme introduction to Richard McCabe as Scapino, a play I interpreted as encouraging to the point of parody the excessive greed and violence of its elder politicians while the trickster himself was being worn to death by his role. This theme, according to Kemp's notes, was then trailed through an entire society in *The Government Inspector.* This, pointedly for Kemp, can be seen as our (New Labour and neo-con) society, where we ourselves enable our political leaders' spin and duplicity. It is Martin Crimp's Hydra principle operating among people generally, to prolong a culture of fear.

Watching *5/11*, after first seeing *The Scarlet Letter*, where the character of Hester refuses the role in which 'society dresses her', I was already aware of how relevant these plays were to what had happened to me since the bombings. I worried continually that any reminder in the play of the terrorist bomb might cause me to have a flashback. I thought about Martin Crimp's comment that we live a privileged existence separated from death and dismemberment. The photograph of Blair at Gleneagles constantly picked at my mind while I watched first the hypocritical mayor of Boston in *The Scarlet Letter*, then (and especially) the scheming pragmatist Lord Cecil in *5/11* and, of course, the Trickster role in *Scapino*.

Between performances I read a newspaper piece by theatre director Dominic Dromgoole, and it helped me pull all the productions together. Without my usual research methodologies, or even the ability to read more than programme notes and newspaper articles, I was responding much more to public professional voices. Dromgoole's theme was that, 'If playwrights really want to get to grips with modern terrorism, they need to switch off the daily news', and he lambasted those who accuse theatre of 'preaching to the converted'. He argued that good theatre does something very different from preaching. It generates 'an odd reaction to the friction between our journey and the facts of the world'. This is not the conspiratorial, childish leftism that news journalists on the right like to ascribe to playwrights like Harold Pinter. (In the *Daily Telegraph* report on 14 October on Pinter's Nobel, Charles Spencer refers to 'these adolescent politics [which] have infiltrated his plays'.) Rather, Dromgoole argues, theatre can open up 'the dust of the moment' for much more general democratic questioning and debate – and it is pretty clear that this for Dromgoole is all about Bush and bin Laden:

> Theatre is a place of imagination, of compassion and of obsession ... It may be useful for dramatists to stop trying to ape journalism's task of making people understand. I think we are all sick of trying to understand the Iraq war. I am sure that nothing amuses George and Dick and Osama more than watching everyone burn all their energy up on understanding, while the three of them carry on merrily dynamiting the foundations of the crumbling palace of enlightenment. We need our theatre, and our art, to stop understanding, and to help us jump forward. Our greatest theatre, from Aeschylus

through Shakespeare and Chekhov and O'Casey, has been about creating a new idea of the human.

I wondered if, thinking through Dromgoole's ideas at Chichester, audiences could experience, between their enforced silence over Iraq and the theatre's return to it, not so much understanding but a feeling of empowerment.

How, though, does this work? As I watched *5/11*, I saw it combining the religious and economic deconstruction of the other two plays I'd just seen, digging deeper into my psyche. I agreed with Michael Billington's review comment on 20 August that in the play 'Catesby trying to extract from the cautious Jesuit leader, Henry Garnett, intellectual justification for acts of terror' was a powerful moment that was not only explained by the economics and religion of a period in English history, but speaks insistently to our present time, since 'while Kemp topically suggests that the Gunpowder Plot was a disproportionate response to persecution that would have killed the innocent along with the guilty, he also argues that a state that reneges on promised multiculturalism invites disaster.'

I watched *5/11* immediately after reading Kemp's programme notes for *Scapino*, *The Scarlet Letter* and *The Government Inspector*. As I sat there, the exploration of personal guilt (over political betrayal) and the cascading spin justifying state and individual terror had many obvious and deliberate parallels to Iraq and the 'war against terror'. As I saw it, *5/11* was focusing on a number of the things about Iraq that had been worrying me:

- The issue of torture – Kemp wrote that, 'officially forbidden by Magna Carta (the Human Rights Act of its day), [torture] was frequently developed in cases of national sovereignty, and we have the King's authorisation for its use on Fawkes'. Kemp also implicitly refers to Guantánamo Bay and Abu Ghraib in noting that a 'man under torture (which might include sleep deprivation and drugs as well as the rack and thumbscrews) may confess to almost anything'.

- Government spin of evidence over the weapon of mass destruction of that age: gunpowder.
- Government manipulation of the ideology of multiculturalism, employing – as it suits politicians – both the climate-of-fear inflation of Catholic numbers (read Muslim threat) and the rhetorical division of Catholics into the 'good, not guilty' and 'terrorist'.
- Presidential-style politicians (the powerfully pragmatic Cecil in *5/11*).
- The construction of statesmanship as a combination of spin, terror-manipulation, economic control and suborning of the law in the mixing of politics with law through key discussions with the attorney general.
- Rhetorical justification for the terrorising and killing of innocents.
- The creative ability of paranoid pragmatists in government (Cecil in *5/11* perceives springtime British tulips as an endless landscape of 'imams in their turbans').

All of these themes Kemp referred to in the play nagged away at my thinking as I watched and when I discussed the play with Marian afterwards. They engaged me physically, too, in my own gut reaction to the flashes of light and to the very bloody forms of torture and the shocking hangings at the conclusion of the play. Watching this historical reconstruction, I felt powerfully an awareness that terrorism was not other but was deep in our culture. As Kemp emphasises, 'a play is not a history lesson and I am writing ... to interpret events in the light of contemporary concerns'.

Just how contemporary? Between his actual writing of the programme notes and the publication of his introduction to the script, the terrorist attacks of 7/7 had happened, so that the four young men of 7 July now slipped into what Kemp wrote next:

> What interests me as much as the activities of thirteen young men in 1605 are the recurring patterns which may link them to nineteen young men in 2001 [the 9/11 terrorists], or four young men in 2005 [the 7/7 terrorists], or thirteen young men in the early years of the first millennium [there is an explicit 'Christ at his Last Supper' staging of the thirteen Gunpowder conspirators in *5/11*], or any number of the disillusioned or the dispossessed who have chosen to use religion to bind themselves together in blood. The very unreasonableness of faith, which can be its great glory in speaking truth to power, has too often made its own assertions of authority particularly barbaric.

Most importantly, what Kemp's *5/11* reminded me, and maybe its audiences, was that religious barbarity lies not only in the Muslim world, nor even only across the Atlantic in the contemporary fundamentalist US. It resides in British mainstream (Catholic/Protestant) history as recently as the terrorism of 1605, and as foundationally as Christ's Last Supper. As Kemp emphasises, this recognition within Christianity itself – of the barbarous underbelly of our own mythical stories of resistance and heroic martyrdom – should sink us, deeply and reflexively, into uncertainty and ambivalence, because the 'very imperviousness to suffering that the early Christians showed in the arena before the lions . . . is now what we find so frightening in the face of the jihad . . . played out in a country trying to find an identity in a world where the border between religion and the state is being redrawn'.

Now theatre like this may be deemed of the left (usually by those on the right), but it is in no way preaching to the converted. It is, though, aiming at personal change, because it is above all aware of the terrorising stories (or spin) constructed everywhere in our lives – by artists, by actors, by Blairite political leaders-as-actors, by religious fundamentalists, by heroes and by terrorists, and also by ourselves as observers and audiences, as we allow ourselves to be duped by what Kemp calls the tricksters' 'fragmentary speech'.

Pace Tony Blair, not 'everything has changed' since 7/7. Indeed, most of it has happened before. And maybe (to use Nagy's words) our 'quite constructive' response to guilt, when confronted by the international oppression that encourages terrorism, is to follow Hester's 'frank refusal to bear [it] (as opposed to the penalty)'; to grow sick with Scapino of ritually conforming with political falsity and duplicity; and to continue resisting (especially as we vote) the political manipulation of evidence, the national denial of human rights acts, the realpolitik myths of multiculturalism (dividing us between 'moderate' and 'extreme' Islamists) and the parliamentary and media construction of statesmanship in the face of terror.

The point I am making is that British alienation is not just fertile ground among extremists and 'mad mullahs' in Muslim cultures. It is everywhere. It formulates the very language of professional intellectuals working in so many different spheres in the UK (whom I have chosen to represent in this chapter by those working in the theatre). As the first of two concluding examples, here is theatre reviewer Susannah Clapp on 8 May 2005 in the *Observer*:

> When Nicholas Hytner took over as artistic director [of the National Theatre] just before the invasion of Iraq, he directed a dynamic modern-dress *Henry V* which shattered the play's patriotic core, showing a war waged on a shabby pretext, a nation of reluctant conscripts led by an imperfect warrior-king. Now, in the midst of a general election, he has staged the infinitely more searching *Henry IV* plays

and shaken his audience all over again. This shock is different and deeper. These plays can't be reduced to an issue: they are both more panoramic and more personal; they conjure up alternative ideas of what Britain has been, and will fail to be. In the course of six hours you travel through epochs.

And here is the distinguished academic Jonathan Bate writing in the programme for the Hammersmith Lyric's *Julius Caesar*:

> To what degree should political power be concentrated in a single leader? Is the democratic process strong enough to withstand a potential tyrant or are there times when direct action on the street is the only possible course of action? Can we trust politicians to serve the people rather than their own interests? *Julius Caesar* is alive and full of troubling force in the early twenty-first century.

Bate's notes make a direct analogy between Shakespeare's time, post-Armada, and our own time, post-9/11, as he writes that this earlier England – comparably with the US's neo-conservative stance after the collapse of the Soviet bloc – having seen off Spain, had the 'potential to become the greatest empire in the modern world'. In this context, Lord Essex, looking back to the imperial Roman model of power, planned, says Bates, his own shock and awe campaign against Irish insurgents in 1599 (the year in which *Julius Caesar* was written).

The point is that we are not just talking here about the individual interpretation of theatre plays. Nor are we only talking about what Dominic Dromgoole calls 'journalism's task of making people understand'. It goes well beyond that to a public discourse circulating throughout Britain – in its theatres, in significant parts of the media, in academia, among writers and art critics – which is insisting, as he says, that we now jump forward (well past our spinning politicians and tabloids) to create 'a new idea of the human' that focuses on the complex and uncertain questions we are all asking about freedom and civil liberties in the face of those who threaten them now more clearly than ever we remember.

Bad theatre

Two events that occurred in September and October, 2005, indicated clearly the binaries that historian Joanna Bourke wrote about in the *Guardian* on 1 October: about the political reconstruction of a culture of fear opposed by an international recognition of a culture of ethical responsibility.

The first event was a piece of bad theatre at the New Labour Party conference in Brighton. Walter Wolfgang, an eighty-two-year-old man who had been a member of the party for fifty-seven years, was forcibly ejected in full view of the TV cameras after calling out 'Nonsense' when Jack Straw spoke from the stage about New Labour's progress in bringing democracy to Iraq.

This wasn't the only bad theatre at Brighton that week. The entire conference was stage-managed to such a degree that no debate was allowed at all on Iraq. Yet this one issue has fundamentally split the party and led thousands of its members to feel a sense of complete powerlessness. In his piece in the *Observer* on 2 October, 'Why I'm Tearing Up My Labour Party Card', the internationally respected film and media scholar Colin McCabe wrote: 'If Nazi Germany was fascism by radio, New Labour is the corporate state by television. The determination to control the party's image on television is incompatible with a democratic party, and indeed with a democracy.' Referring to the treatment of Walter Wolfgang, after Iraq, McCabe said in a direct riposte to Blair, 'it is clear that you yourself have no belief in any goal of real equality – the new Labour aim, Brown as well as Blair, is just to manage the underclass. Of course, there can be no debate' – hence the symptomatic treatment of long-term party loyalists like Walter Wolfgang.

Similarly, in the *Guardian* on 30 September, Polly Toynbee – who had encouraged us to vote New Labour with a 'clothes-peg on your nose' in April 2005 – wrote a piece, 'This Strangulation of Dreams is Creating a Phantom Party'. It began:

> The symbolism was too good to be true. No screenwriter could have devised so apt an image as the rough handling of an 82-year-old party member out of the Labour conference for shouting 'That's a lie!' Some New Labour enthusiasts have scoffed at such a triviality getting front page display, but they deliberately ignore its graphic significance. The old man perfectly embodied a weak and depleted party that was not even allowed to debate the war it has been dragged into. It hasn't been necessary yet to forcibly eject all members from the party: half have already stomped off of their own accord. The hall in Brighton was emptier than for years: two thirds of MPs did not bother to attend and a third of constituencies failed to send any delegates . . . Who cares about the state of the parties? Certainly not the 40% of the public who didn't vote. Manufactured applause, archaic speeches and arcane composite motions make conferences look like some obscure religious rite behind an altar screen.

Very many people that I know are as appalled as Colin McCabe and Polly Toynbee (and Toynbee found many, many more as she stopped during the election campaign at many traditional Labour voters' front doors) that Blair has, in McCabe's words, 'told the world, to this country's enduring risk and shame, that Britain will back any American government, no matter how dangerous, in pursuing reckless schemes of military adventure'. In doing this, as he says to Blair, 'you despise all the Labour party's best traditions'.

Good theatre

The second event occurred a couple of weeks later on 13 October, when it was announced that British playwright Harold Pinter had been awarded the Nobel Prize for Literature. The following morning, the *Independent* gave its front cover to a piece by Pinter, 'We Have Brought Torture and Misery in the Name of Freedom'. In an extract from a speech Pinter had originally given when winning the Wilfred Owen Award earlier in 2005, the playwright says:

> The great poet Wilfred Owen articulated the tragedy, the horror – and indeed the pity – of war in a way that no other poet has. Yet we have learnt nothing. Nearly 100 years after his death the world has become more savage, more brutal, more pitiless ... What would Owen have made of the invasion of Iraq? A bandit act, an act of blatant state terrorism, demonstrating absolute contempt for the concept of International Law. An arbitrary military action inspired by a series of lies upon lies and gross manipulation of the media and therefore of the public. An act intended to consolidate American military and economic control of the Middle East masquerading – as a last resort (all other justifications having failed to justify themselves) – as liberation.

Pinter ended the piece, 'Wilfred Owen would share our contempt, our revulsion, our nausea and our shame at both the language and the actions of the American and British governments', and it is his challenge to the use and misuse of language that is emphasised in the Nobel citation, which speaks of Pinter's work as uncovering 'the precipice under everyday prattle and forc[ing] entry into oppression's closed rooms'. In this sense there is a strong continuity between Pinter's early and his later, supposedly political theatre and poetry. His biographer Michael Billington, writing in the *Guardian* on 14 October, noted that 'Pinter's constant campaign against the devaluation of language – particularly words like "freedom" and "democracy" – and his moral opposition to the abuse of human rights, has been internationally recognised'.

In response to Pinter's Nobel award, another British playwright, David Harc, wrote:

> It is perhaps the most depressing feature of the powerful democratic movement against the Iraq invasion that no major figures have come out of that movement who have been able to articulate in any powerful way the deep sense of betrayal and anger that has marked the most dangerous and dishonourable of wars. For almost 20 years now, Harold has been – often at considerable personal cost – the most prominent spokesperson in this country for those who are hapless victims of belligerence and oppression. Like Arundhati Roy, he has worked to begin to define what in uniquely dangerous times, we may expect an artist to be.

I agree with Hare's notion of the artist, in what are indeed uniquely dangerous times for our own and other democracies. And so does Martin Jacques in his programme notes for the Lyric Theatre, Hammersmith, production of *Julius Caesar* in September/October 2005 – a performance which also strongly emphasised the relationship between political language, media spin and the death of democracy. In the notes,

Jacques argues that far from democracy being a kind of universal truth – as is endlessly conveyed in US and British government propaganda – in fact, 'History and culture leaves an indelible imprint on the possibilities and nature of any democracy'.

He points to significant differences between, for example, Japanese one-party faction democracy, Britain's 'plutocracy mediated by democracy' and Berlusconi's mediacracy in Italy:

> The Western model of democracy, like everything else, is a distinct phase in history, which depends upon certain conditions for its existence . . . There are grounds for believing that Western democracy, as we have known it, is in decline. The symptoms [are] . . . the decline of parties, the fall in turnout, the decline in politics as a societal activity, a growing disregard for politics and politicians, the displacement of politics from the centre stage of politics to its wings.

The decline in electoral turnout, as well as the increase in presidential-style leadership via informal sofa cabinets, becomes a crucial issue, as when we claim, 'Not in my name, Tony Blair' over the Iraq war. Jacques clearly agrees with Polly Toynbee on the risk to democracy that we face, and his explanation of these symptoms is disturbing:

> The rise of the modern labour movement . . . served to provide societies with real choice: instead of the logic of the market, it offered a different philosophy, different values, a different kind of society and a different narrative. Even the funding of these parties was different: they enjoyed little support from big business, instead relying on trade unions and individual mobilisation. The decline of traditional social-democratic parties – as illustrated by New Labour – has meant the erosion of choice, at least in any profound sense of

the term. Politics has moved onto singular ground: that of the market. Voting, as a result, has become that much less meaningful.

The Lyric's performance of *Julius Caesar*, running in September, was all about the virtual politics of media imaging, and the loss of democracy. I agree with Jacques' reading of the performance as not simply referring to the post-Soviet bloc or to Berlusconi's Italy (which are its overt references), but to the entire West. And whether we agree or not with Jacques' particular interpretation of *Julius Caesar* – and the appearance of his views at length in the official programme notes for the production certainly gives them extra credibility – what they also indicate is that David Hare's pessimism about the few artists and intellectuals who have voiced their anger over the Iraq war may be misplaced. British theatre over the past two years – in Greek tragedies, Shakespearean histories and contemporary plays on terrorism, spin and the new wars – has consistently tried to empower by giving us 'a voice in the democratic process'. This has been a major challenge to those politicians who articulate the culture of terror.

NINE

Different Media, Different Voices

Media requests for interviews came at me thick and fast over the six months after 7 July. At a certain point my self-defined role in them began to shift from being victim to researcher, because I now knew that I had a book to write for Little, Brown. Soon the media also began to show interest in the idea of an academic media analyst whose image was appearing so regularly. It became a new angle, so that even on 2 January 2006 in a short interview on the Australian commercial radio station 2UE, the interviewer Peter Fitzsimmons asked me first about my experiences on 7 July, but then asked, 'As a professor of media studies, was it extraordinary for you to go from being an expert at the way the media works to being the story itself?'

The turning point for the media in respect of my dual identity as victim and expert was when the *Sun* newspaper used my image on its front page in November 2005 to support Tony Blair's anti-terror legislation. For me personally, though, I had thought about this and how I would respond to interviews much earlier, in October, when I also began to think about writing this book.

My first engagement came on 7 October, three months on from the bombings. The intention, which I had discussed with my sons in July, remained very important: I wanted to get across a citizen's as well as a victim's viewpoint. But there was now a difference. I had recovered enough, albeit slowly, to perceive these things more analytically, and to observe from the inside the way different media used, or indeed excluded, public voices. This phase of my recovery was positive for me personally and politically, too, because I started to explore the many good things (as well as some bad) about the British media. Most media professionals would say that the different voices of the public are important to the workings of democracy. But how, and in what ways, do they facilitate this? In some cases, as I found in the press and in British theatre, voices did raise questions that were central to civic engagement on the issue of the Iraq war. However, most of the time these questioning voices were influenced by the practices of professionals working in the media, as I found at BBC Radio Five Live in September 2005.

Matthew Bannister explores . . .

On 7 October, Five Live broadcast two programmes marking three months on from the terror attacks. During that week they had been running a series of interviews, with telephone and email feedback, under the concept of pairing experiences. So on Thursday, 6 October they chaired a discussion between someone who lost her mother to an IRA bomb in 1987 and a woman who lost her sister on 7/7. On Friday, 7 October at 10.05 a.m., they ran part of a discussion between Craig Staniforth and myself (recorded earlier), followed by a discussion with me in the studio.

Craig and I had met to record quite a long interview the week before. The producer gave me a list of questions and asked me to play the interviewer with Craig, while adding my own responses. It was an excellent concept professionally, because it led to a mutual discussion, yet from different points of view and without interruption by an interviewer.

It was also fascinating for me personally, because I learned a number of things that I either didn't know before or had forgotten; for example, how Craig trains his colleagues now to deal with emergencies without all the sophisticated equipment they have at base.

Radio Five Live put the full interview on its website, and used about five minutes of it – the discussion of what happened in the train – on air on 7 October. Victoria Derbyshire then talked with me about my time with Craig, how long it took the emergency services to come, and how I felt, three months on. I avoided talking about wider considerations because I was going to be on a Five Live discussion the same evening, when political issues might come up (I was already wondering how to deal with that).

Therefore, there were two taxi rides for me that day to the BBC's White City studios. In between these, the clothes I wore on 7/7 were returned to me by the bomb squad, the *News of the World* visited me and I did a radio interview with BBC Wales' *Drive Time*. It was a busy and emotionally fraught day. As I was not sleeping well at night, I was tired by the time I got back, at 10.05 p.m., to the Five Live studios for the second programme. The discussion was with a group of people most of whom had direct experiences of 7/7: John Faulding, who had lost his Israeli partner; Tony Blacker, a London taxi driver who had broken the news on 7 July of the Aldgate bombing to Matthew Bannister on Five Live; Sarfraz Manzoor, a Muslim writer and documentary film-maker; Eileen Quinton, who lost her mother in the Enniskillen IRA bombings of 1987 and now raises awareness of the effects of terrorist trauma; and Jamal el-Shayal, a young Muslim student activist who had done research on extremism and the causes of the bombings. This selection of speakers was consistent with Five Live's morning programmes that week, Eileen, Jamal and myself having all been involved in the pairing interviews.

I had checked out in advance the *Radio Times* description of the programme to give myself a sense of its agenda:

> 10.00 London Bombings – the Way Forward. Matthew Bannister explores the devastating impact of the four suicide explosions that brought death and destruction to London on July 7.

The blurb noted that the programme would profile people deeply affected, physically and/or emotionally, and invite them to compare their experiences with those who had suffered from other terrorist attacks. And it would include a discussion with Muslim speakers about racial hatred since the July bombs.

Now sitting in the radio studio, I was conscious that I was there as writer as well as victim. This dual identity raised problems for me. Ethically, it was my normal practice to tell any media that interviewed me that I was writing a book about my experiences, which would include writing about my interaction with them – and I had done that on Five Live that morning. Methodologically, the problem was harder because I wanted to talk about the wider political issues but at the same time as an academic knew that a more ethnographic approach, allowing the round-table discussion to flow naturally, would work well. Of course, as a social scientist, I also knew that there is no such thing as natural research – or natural media discussion for that matter – that it always involves a power relationship (between interviewer and interviewee) and that good ethnographic research needs to take this into consideration.

This is what I tried to do that night, though I was tired after such a busy day. My physical condition back then (and still now) meant I was prone to sudden, extreme bouts of tiredness, which cut in like heavy jet lag, and I felt like that on the evening of the discussion. This may have been a good thing, because it did make me less garrulous than usual, able to sit back a little and observe the interviewer's professional role in orchestrating the flow between participants.

Matthew Bannister opened the conversation by asking the two anchor members of the panel, John and Sarfraz (who would be there throughout the programme's two hours), to speak about the effect 7/7 had had on them, and how they had responded. John spoke of how his loss had led to him becoming incredibly busy, as he wrote thousands of words into a diary remembering the details of his life with his girlfriend and speculating on the things they might have done had she lived. He had also been seeing friends of hers whom he had not met before. Sarfraz said that at the time of the bomb he had been afraid that his personal and his cultural life as a Muslim would be unalterably changed. He felt this even more after the 21 July attacks, because he saw them as the beginning of 'a pattern, a wave of bombings' that would have very negative effects on security and Muslim community relations. Three months on, though, he was back to travelling on the Tube, and, partly as a result of London mayor Ken Livingstone's post-7/7 emphasis on one multicultural city, he was feeling optimistic.

Matthew turned next to the eyewitnesses of 7/7. Tony Blacker described his feelings that day, and his attempts to persuade his traumatised family to go on catching the Tube and buses, which they were still very uncomfortable doing. Although the increased use of taxis since the attacks is positive from his work point of view, he still tries to get people to carry on and resist terrorism by using public transport as well.

My turn as witness came next. After describing what happened on the Circle Line train and my short-term targets towards recovery afterwards, I was asked about the bigger psychological aspect of what happened to me. Did I have time to feel anger, or think about who had done it and caused all of this hurt that I was suffering? I gave a cautious and muted response, saying that I'd had plenty of time to feel anger in my hospital bed, but that as an academic I'd also had time to see the way in which the media were debating it: the search for those who had done it, the discussion about why it had happened, the issue of Iraq, 'so there was plenty of time for me to go through different feelings of anger'. I was avoiding the direct question, but Matthew wouldn't let me get away with that: 'And that was anger against the perpetrators?' I replied that I didn't particularly feel anger against the perpetrators, but felt sadness when I saw the pictures of the terrorists' families.

Matthew then turned to John Faulding and asked whether he had felt anger against the perpetrators who had deprived him of his loved one. John's response was, 'No, not at all. I saw them immediately as victims. I felt anger, or tried to feel anger against whoever had manipulated them. But . . . their families have to some extent suffered more because they have lost a loved one . . . and they have to live for ever with the consequences of what their loved one did to humanity.'

Matthew responded, 'Well, I have to say that's an incredibly reassuring point of view, and maybe quite a surprising one for me to hear, because I would have expected you and John Tulloch to feel anger and want retribution for something that . . . you are innocent victims of. Can you explain, perhaps, to people listening why you don't feel that anger?' John Faulding responded that it may have been an inbuilt mechanism with him, since anger was an emotional response that expended energy. Rather, he wanted 'to try to come to terms with this in a more rational way, to cling on to whatever religiosity I have, and try to find forgiveness'.

Matthew asked me if I shared that view. I responded that I also saw them as victims, that they were part of complex situations that I didn't have answers for, and that there were major political players strutting around who I felt were more the culprits than those people. John was nodding his head vigorously beside me as I said this, and Matthew said, 'So you thought that the politicians in some way were to blame for this situation?', to which I gave the muted response, 'You can say that, yes.'

What I was doing, under interviewer pressure, was giving Matthew a cue, without pushing it, to extend the discussion, to see what he would do with it. I had the feeling that in this part of the round table dedicated to eyewitnesses and victims, he didn't want to push that, so I (as researcher) didn't either. As a good chair, Matthew turned immediately to someone who hadn't spoken yet, the 1987 IRA victim (and now trauma adviser) Eileen, asking her for her comments on what John and I had said. Eileen said that in relation to anger, her personal experience was that the perpetrators had been less important to her than her lost mother, so they just didn't figure in her consciousness until other people started to mention it. But, responding to John Faulding's comment about forgiveness, she said that her anger came 'because there was so much talk about forgiveness around Enniskillen that it was almost in reaction against that – because I personally don't believe in forgiving people who aren't sorry'.

Matthew, an alert chair, turned to Sarfraz with, 'I think you wanted to raise a point about the earlier discussion.' Sarfraz emphasised that John's and my discussion about not feeling hatred was reassuring, but as a Muslim after 7/7 he did 'actually feel, if not hatred, frustration with the people who did it, not only for what they did, but also for the fact that what they did was also twist and project a certain form of Islam as being the mainstream view . . . So that immediately after that Islam was on the back foot and had to be defended.'

After a break, Matthew Bannister turned back to Eileen,

saying that while the two Johns had been talking about what things were like for them now, three months on, what was it like for her eighteen years on? Eileen said that the pain lasts a long time, and only recently had she got enough information to know the details of what actually happened to her mother. She added that other people seemed to own her mother's death, for example over the details of the memorial. Because Eileen was being critical of the professional and administrative takeover in 1987, Matthew Bannister turned to John and me to ask whether we had received good professional care. We were both very positive about the support of the police and other services, and, in my case, of the media as well in the form of the Mentorn documentary team.

Matthew then turned to Jamal, who had not yet been given the opportunity to speak, raising again Sarfraz's comment about his anger with the terrorists. Jamal responded that his first feeling was that the terrorists had wrecked four years of his work in getting more representation for Muslims in community relations. The response of the mayor had been positive, but the media, in order to sell papers, then fell away from their emphasis on the multicultural nature of the people killed to one on the bombers as evil terrorists. Jamal and his sister could easily have been on the Russell Square train, so it was very frustrating to see the shift away from positive attitudes and how we could move ahead.

To bring back in the pairing aspect of Five Live's programming, Matthew read an email from a young Muslim expressing anger with the terrorists for creating problems for him on the Underground, then asked Jamal whether he and his friends felt they were more likely to be searched now. Jamal confirmed this. For the first couple of weeks after 7/7, he didn't carry a rucksack. Later, there was an incident when another passenger was staring at his bag. 'You just want to open up your bag to show that there's nothing there, but there might be an undercover cop who will shoot you ... The fright was for the future, that unless we actually came together, unless there was the same sense shared by the people here today, that actually we wouldn't get through this. And like people say, when 21 July happened . . . that's when I think it really did kick in . . . The response after 7/7 was a million times better than it was after 9/11, but after 21/7 the media got worse.' The issue of racial hatred, incited by the media, had been raised and was to come and go throughout the programme.

At this moment, it was clear that the problem of incitement formed part of what Jamal wanted to discuss, namely four things – socio-economic deprivation in the Muslim community, resentment over double standards in government foreign policy, the lack of understanding the bombers had about their own religion, and the role of the media. These came out of his study of Muslim youth, and would have been a good basis for discussion over the next hour of the programme.

But the media, even when operating well as I believe it was at Five Live that evening, don't work like that. This programme had an advertised remit in advance: 'Three Months On: London Bombings – the Way Forward'. It will have had producer-guided and sequenced sections for its two-hour round table planned in advance: in this case, 'victims and eyewitnesses', 'tourism', 'security on public transport' and 'intelligence – stopping the terrorists'. Matthew's role as interviewer was to guide us through these sequences and through the other pre-planned structures of the programme, such as its clear determination to introduce a cross-section of Muslim opinion, and to link up with the pairing interviews of the week.

Matthew's remit will have been tight. His focus was the bombings and how to go forward from July. To this, he was also bound to bring his own signature. In his case this appeared early, in the first part of the interview. When both Sarfraz and Jamal were stressing the urgency of exploring why some young Muslims found themselves in such a state of mind that they

could be manipulated to want to do these things, Matthew interrupted: 'The suggestion that there might be someone who wants
to manipulate them makes it more sinister in a way, doesn't it,
because four individuals who go nuts and do this kind of thing
is four individuals who go nuts. But the idea that there is a more
organised plan behind it is much more sinister.'

Jamal replied: 'That's very one-dimensional to say that there's
one person out there. I would say that there's actually at least
four different factors [in] it.' Jamal's four agenda items, coming
out of his own research and potentially broadening our debate,
were replaced here by Matthew's four individuals who go nuts,
and this latter became a recurring motif behind the chair's
sequencing of his questions. It happened with different groups
of experts throughout the discussion.

Some experts, and some sequences, turned out to be much
easier to manage than others in terms of the programme's practical focus on how to go forward from the bombings. I noticed
how comfortably and professionally Matthew managed the
tourism sequence near the end of the hour I was in the studio.
This went seamlessly, with him introducing the topic via his
interviewer from Five Live *Money*, who was standing next to the
London Eye. We heard him talk to a tourism agent who emphasised that it was British tourists who have become anxious
visiting London. Right on cue, the reporter then interviewed
some ladies from Barnsley. They were determined to visit
London and would spent lots· of money there at Christmas,
giving Matthew the chance for a joke about people from
Barnsley with more money than sense. There followed a concluding confirmation from the taxi driver on the panel about
tourism picking up, and the item was over.

This would have been a satisfying section for Matthew and
his team. It was tightly linked to the programme brief, without
any diversionary comment about Iraq (unlike the next segment
of the programme). It was also economically pointed (including

recorded interviews at tourist destination stores like Hamleys) and had some good vox pop with Eileen, Pam, Eunice and Gillian from Barnsley. It offered a little light, inoffensive humour in a programme that wouldn't have many such moments over its two hours. Matthew's role as professional co-ordinator was working well.

In the next item, on London transport security, he had to work harder. His focus here was again the way ahead, with Bob Crow, the general secretary of the RMT, the rail workers' union, who was asked questions within his expertise. Could anything be done technically to stop terrorism on the Underground, and were the bosses cooperating with him? BBC interviewers have lots of experience dealing with union issues and are perfectly comfortable with the combative trench warfare language used, and Matthew was able to chuckle comfortably when Bob twice said that after 7/7 disappeared over the horizon, London Underground bosses went back to their caves and their trenches. However, halfway through the item, Bob suddenly punctured Five Live's tight theme by departing from the agenda. He said, at King's Cross Station:

> Where you've got . . . six exits . . . It's not like where people single-queue and put their bags through. The actual stations are massive open spaces . . . I don't think that's [going to work] at all. What they should be looking at is the political reasons why we face these bombs . . . and that's because of the government's involvement in the illegal war in Iraq.

Matthew's response was immediate and diversionary: 'Right, well, we'll come to that a little later in the programme. But I wanted to focus if I may on the more practical side of what your members would like to see.' His words 'your members' say it all: Bob was there as a union leader rather than a citizen, just as I was there as victim. Politics would be dealt with elsewhere in the programme, and Matthew led Bob back to talking about metal detectors and bosses.

Following the end of this segment, there was an interesting exchange as Matthew turned to his remaining studio guests, John and Sarfraz, to bring them back into the conversation: 'John Faulding, you're smiling at that.' John said that he was not altogether in agreement with Bob that there could not be higher-level security surveillance in the Underground.

John: Well, millions and millions of people would stop carrying rucksacks and briefcases, because if you didn't have a case you would go straight through [metal detectors]. Ideally, you would then open your coat to a security guard to make sure you didn't have a belt of explosives, and it would be in a short space of time quite self-regulating.

Matthew: Mm. Do you think that's a good idea, Sarfraz?

Sarfraz: I think if there was a visible presence, that would be more likely to do something rather than gates and searches and things. The second is I remember reading you could do a sort of body scan as you went through the tunnels. But I kind of agree with Bob Crow actually that if you're going to stop it, you're not going to stop it by investing billions of pounds in the Underground. It's much more about grass-roots reasons for why any [terrorist] would get to King's Cross in the first place.

A couple of things interest me about this part of the round-table discussion. The first is that in between the pre-planned segments some open discussion by participants as citizens (i.e., not John simply as victim or Sarfraz as Muslim film-maker) breaks out as a result of another aspect of the programme's structure (i.e., the role of the anchoring guests, John and Sarfraz). The second is that here the guests decide to engage directly with what Bob Crow had said. In this way, a public debate about practical security issues in the Underground was opened up, and might have gone further in a sustained round-table discussion. I had left the studio at 11 p.m., but if I had still been there I would have asked about the introduction of sniffer dogs, which have been promised but are nowhere visible, and I might have suggested that Bob Crow's ideas be debated much more widely. For example, why not ask the travelling public to discuss the apparently insurmountable problem of the number of exits and entrances at Tube stations? Perhaps some of these – or even whole stations – might be closed in order to be able to provide high-tech security at the others. Maybe the London public might choose to walk further between stations if they felt safer when they got there. Or maybe not – but my point is that this discussion could be taken much further in the media and elsewhere. In the absence of these citizens' voices being taken seriously as experts in themselves, media (as in the *Sun* example I will talk about) tend to extend the culture of fear from above.

The issue of Iraq had been brought up four times in the programme thus far. It had been introduced obliquely by me, then as an agenda item of causes by Jamal, overtly by Bob, and implicitly in Sarfraz's support for Bob in seeing grass-roots reasons for terrorism on the London Underground. Around 11.30 p.m., the Five Live round table moved into its final segment, about intelligence and 'how to stop the bombers'. This was always likely to be where Iraq would be discussed. The segment had two kinds of input. First, Charles Shoebridge, a former counter-terrorism officer, and Dr Sandra Bell, Director of Homeland Security and Resilience at the Royal United Services Institute, spoke about mistakes made by intelligence before 7/7 and how improvements had been implemented, or else were still needed in the security framework. Second, Sarfraz was now joined by Harris Bokhari from the Muslim Association of Britain, who continued to debate the root causes of the London bombings, while Matthew continued with his signature line.

Matthew: If four people are going to go nuts and blow people up on the Tube . . . I don't see why you should be able to do anything about it.

Harris responded: 'Forget intelligence or no intelligence, the war in Iraq was an issue. It doesn't matter how many times Tony Blair wants to hide or bury it, or the government wants to hide and bury it.'

This statement led to the biggest flurry of interruption and cross-talking in the entire two hours, as both Harris and Matthew tried to protest across the other's comments.

Matthew: But hang on a second, you can't have it both ways. You can't say that these people have a legitimate political griev-ance, and when they go and blow up they are nutty people who are completely outside your community.

Harris: No. These acts were totally unjustified, let me correct that. To defend Bob Crow here – we are not saying this is a legitimate reason to do these acts, of course not, they are dis-gusting acts – but then we have to understand what is the core root problem of this . . . we have to sort out our foreign policies, we have to make sure we are not hated in the world any more.

Matthew: But we shouldn't have to change our foreign policies because four nuts blow up people on the Tube. We shouldn't have to do that. That would be giving in to the terrorists, wouldn't it?

Harris: Not at all. We should make sure we are not investing millions and billions of pounds outside the UK in a foreign war when we could be investing into our schools and hospitals in this country. We should be investing that in our youth in this coun-try. Why do we have disenfranchised youth in all communities in all races? Let's fund it into them, let's make sure that our youth grow up with a correct understanding of their religion, the cor-rect understanding of what it means to be a citizen in this country. And make sure they integrate in a positive way. And that's through funding things like youth centres, youth work, helping out kids in the street.

At this point, Matthew turned, perhaps for a balancing com-ment, to Sarfraz, who did feel that Harris should get out of the mosques and schools a bit more to look for terrorists who 'may slip under the radar'. But he, too, disagreed with Matthew, asking to bring the conversation back to 'the root causes, which Jamal mentioned I think quite interestingly an hour ago . . . they haven't gone away. So it seems to be self-evident that . . . because none of the reasons, whether they be politics, whether they be integration questions, have been solved in the last three months, so why should we assume it's not going to happen again?'

By the end of the two-hour round table, there was some consensus that preventing more terrorism depended at one level on continuing intelligence through the chain of contact with Muslim communities and at another on surveillance of the indoctrination/recruitment and supply of explosives to young British Muslim men. What the programme had not got very far in discussing, though, was the way forward in respect of Jamal's four core issues. Matthew turned gloomily to Charles: 'People seem to be assuming that there could be another attack. Is London the likely target?' Charles responded that though London has a symbolic advantage for terrorists, if fifty-two people were killed in Milton Keynes or Bishop's Stortford it would still make headlines around the world. 'And of course, people are saying, "I'm not going to use the Tube." But it could be a shopping centre or a bowling alley, anywhere where people congregate. Everybody is at risk from this kind of terrorism.' And, on that sombre message, Matthew closed the round-table discussion. He had explored his brief very professionally, and sitting there listening to him I was becoming aware of both the advantages of open debate between equals and the disadvantages of category-driven constraints (as expert or victim) in this kind of media forum.

Doorstepped?

As well as going through the familiar cycle of victims and helpers, the tragic and dead, and finding the bad guys, any major media coverage of a disaster looks for new angles in order to recycle the story. And so the British media went through their cycle: 7/7; 21/7; the killing of Jean Charles de Menezes coupled with the capture of the four would-be bombers from 21/7; the retrospectives of 7/7 at one, two, three and six months afterwards; the emerging issue of compensation in September and October; the St Paul's memorial service on 1 November; the government's defeat over the ninety-day arrest-without-charge legislation in mid-November; the refusal of the government in December to appoint an independent inquiry into 7/7; and the end-of-year summaries in late December 2005.

By October, I was already exhausted by exposure to this cycle, so I was trying to lie low again. However, many media outlets were trying to contact me for my views about the compensation issue. My first response was that I had little to say. Nonetheless, I raised this with my publishers, who were now moving towards announcing the book, and they thought that some contact with the media might help. In particular, aware of the amount of exposure I was getting in reviews on 7 October, three months after the attacks, they suggested I might speak with the *Evening Standard* and the *News of the World* once the early publicity for the book had been released.

I called both the relevant journalists, saying that while I had huge sympathy and empathy for the deserving cases, like Martine Wright, another victim who had been only a few feet from the bomb (at Aldgate) and had lost both her legs, I didn't have much to say. I suggested that they should interview people who were facing huge costs, whereas I was on sick leave for six months on full salary.

The *News of the World* journalist persevered. She indicated that the newspaper was mounting a campaign against the government on behalf of compensation for victims, and would I give it my blessing? I said, 'Yes', thinking this would be the end of the matter. About a week later, on 7 October – my busy day with

Radio Five Live, BBC Wales and the bomb squad – the publishers rang me to say that the *News of the World* journalist was keen to do an interview that day, but that they would not pass on my phone number to the newspaper unless I wanted them to. I said I didn't, because it was already an emotionally demanding and exhausting day, with the prospect still ahead of me of a full hour's session late that evening at the White City studios.

I thought that was the end of the matter. The phone rang again just a few minutes later. It was Amanda, the *News of the World* journalist, who obviously already had my number. She was asking for a big favour. She was close by with her photographer. All she needed was a few minutes for something to support their campaign. Rather than give a straight 'No', I prevaricated, saying I was too busy because of the bomb squad's visit. Amanda said they would love to come and take pictures of that. I said, 'No way', so she asked whether they could come before or after the police. And I did support the campaign for the worst injured victims of the bombing, didn't I? I weakened, saying that they could come for a short time after the police visit.

They arrived at about 3 p.m. Before letting them in, I said I needed to know what they wanted and how they were going to use it. They showed me what I thought was a headline, 'What About the Victims?' I got the impression that this would be at the top of an article headed by a collage of photographs of quite a number of victims – a togetherness piece on behalf of those with the worst injuries. When we talked about my situation, both on the phone earlier and on the day, I repeated the same points: I was on full salary until January, so any compensation issue was well ahead of me. The journalist asked what my condition was: would I be back at work in January? I admitted that I needed an ear operation which seemed to be stretching well into the future because of a shortage of available hospital beds, and that I probably did need better hearing to teach and run meetings. Amanda asked whether I worried about that. I answered that I was bound to have some worries, but that my head of school had been very supportive so far, and I expected that to continue. She went on, did I have a mortgage? And when I said I did, Amanda asked would I be able to afford to keep my flat on the half-salary I would get if I was not back at work after six months? I said, no, it was a big mortgage, and that might be the time I looked for compensation. I had told her on the phone that I wasn't sleeping well, and she now asked: was I worrying about work, money and my mortgage? I said that in the middle of the night one always thinks the worst, and sometimes I did worry about these things. But equally I worried about other things – about how I still wasn't sleeping, and also, frankly, about how the media were presenting me.

Then came the picture session. We went outside to a small park, and the photographer busied himself, taking the usual, innumerable shots, while I tried to hide my irritation with the whole thing. Then I noticed something. Amanda, on her mobile while the photographer was at work, had something resting against her legs. It was the 'headline'; and then the penny finally dropped. This was in fact a placard, and any minute now they would be asking me to hold it.

I had only seconds to come to a decision, because the photographer was clearly coming to the end of his sequence. Was I going to jack up and say, 'No'? – which I should have said in the first place. Two arguments were buzzing around in my mind. The first was that I really did want to support Martine Wright and other victims, and I assumed that if I didn't hold the placard my photo would be the odd one out in their collage of victim photographs. The second was that my sons' early arguments about avoiding tabloid-style media in the early strong emotions around 7 July were maybe not so relevant now. This was not about 'moderate' and 'fanatical' Muslims. The *News of the World* campaign was against the government.

I went ahead with the placard shots on those grounds, though I did resist two further requests. The photographer asked me to take off my shoes (the ones that the bomb squad had just brought back, with shrapnel in the right toe) and hold them up for him to photograph. I said, 'No way.' Amanda finally asked me for one more big favour. They were organising a big march of victims to Downing Street the next Friday. Would I be prepared to join them? I said, 'No', and I left them, emphasising to Amanda that I wanted them to indicate that the university had been very supportive thus far, and I expected that to continue, whatever happened. She said, 'Fine.'

The article appeared in the *News of the World* on Sunday, 9 October. It was one column, and featured only me. There I was, at the top of the piece, grimly holding my 'What About the Victims?' placard. There was no comforting photo-collage around me of other victims all doing the same. The headline was 'I'm Living in Fear I'll Go Broke', and the text underneath said the following:

> After his dramatic rescue the haunting image of John's bloodied face shocked the world. Now, much of his hearing is gone, he has severe concussion and vertigo – and the trauma still keeps him awake at nights. John . . . lectures in sociology at Brunel University, Uxbridge, and is on full sick-pay until January. 'But what then?' he said. 'If I'm still not able to work my pay will be halved and I can't pay my mortgage. Every night I wake about 1.15 unable to sleep with all the worry. And I was one of the lucky ones. My heart goes out to those who suffered appalling injuries and need constant ongoing care. I'm so grateful to the *News of the World* campaign.

Well! There was one line of what I had actually said, more or less unprompted, about those who suffered appalling injuries. There were several lines, rewritten, that I had half-said under probing, but always in a context and with qualifying comments which had been entirely omitted in this article. And, of course, there was what I felt was a doorstepping tendency of this journalist. I felt I was more or less pushed into an interview that I didn't want to give.

Compare this with the text of another young journalist with the *Western Mail*, Paul, whom I found waiting outside my flat in Cardiff the day after the *News of the World* piece came out. I had just begun staying by myself in Cardiff to get used to that space again and to build up further confidence. Instead I found another journalist at my front door. Like Amanda, Paul wanted a interview on the theme of compensation. I was fairly brusque, saying that I had nothing to say, had already got burnt on this one, and that I would be prepared see him a few hours later if he had some other story he wanted to write.

Paul did turn up, with a photographer, some hours later, at 5 p.m. He asked about a wide range of issues (including some political ones) in a long interview, took a number of photographs and left. He then published two articles from the interview. On 11 October, he focused on the bomb experience itself ('Welsh [*sic*] Professor of Risk Relives Moment of 7/7 Tube Blast'). The photographs were sensitive, the story tight and interesting, and he got in his compensation slant. In a separate box from the rest of the article (coloured yellow), he wrote:

> John Tulloch last night urged the Government to give proper compensation to those permanently prevented from working by the July atrocities. Mr Tulloch said the case of victims like Martine Wright, who has received just a few thousand pounds compensation despite losing the use of her legs after the attacks, highlighted the need for a proper system of payments. 'The thing that I'm sure everybody was most touched by was that really unfortunate young woman in her 30s. My feeling of closeness to her is that here I am with all my legs

and so on and we were perhaps the only two people who were so close to our respective bombers . . . so I've got enormous sympathy and support for anything she needs.'

This was exactly the same account I had given to the *News of the World*, but with such different results. The next day, Paul published a follow-on piece, once more with sensitive photographs: 'Welsh [*sic*] Professor Caught in London Bomb Tells How He is Rebuilding His Life'. Again, there was a small, separate story in a yellow box. He had asked me my thoughts on the terrorists, particularly in the light of the Mohammad Sidique Khan video, and this time he gave me space to tell a bit of my story:

> Despite his injuries, Professor Tulloch said he felt no anger at the sight of the perpetrator. 'I didn't feel much when I saw him on that video message . . . I feel far more troubled and distressed about seeing the images of those guys' wives and children. It's terribly sad, but I'm not angry. I'm far more angry about the politicians and the other people behind the bombs than the individuals who did it. How they came to do what they did I don't know, but the people we should feel sorry for are the families. What are they supposed to do know? Who will support them now? But I'm not saying what they did was acceptable – it was a horrific act of violence.'

Paul did not record the interview. He took notes on a pad, yet he managed virtually to quote me verbatim. I really did say these things, and I was very pleased (in the light of my *News of the World* experiences) to see my own words. Moreover, Paul had got his compensation story, fairly and accurately quoted, and he had given me a little space for my wider comments. It was a good trade-off, and in my view an example of good journalism.

Meanwhile, the PR department at Brunel University was

having trouble with the local Uxbridge media after the hype surrounding the *News of the World* piece, and some putting out of brush fires was needed, by them and by me. I was still seething when my doorbell rang on Wednesday, 12 October, and I was confronted on the doorstep this time by a journalist and cameraman from *ITV (Wales) News*, wanting to do yet another story about compensation. I had been slightly mollified by the *Western Mail* article, but again said I really had no story, and told them about the *News of the World*. They seemed suitably appalled, and they agreed that they were happy to do a wider coverage. The journalist even asked whether I would like her to pose a question cueing my experience with the *News of the World*, so I went for it, saying I would do it generally, without naming names.

The interview lasted about twenty-five minutes, for a news slot of under three. I didn't expect my (unnamed) *News of the World* story to survive the cutting-room floor. But when I saw it, there it was, still in and surrounded by a tight but general item. Like Paul's photographs, the new camera shots of me at home showed recovery, not just the horrors of the attacks. Again, I thought that was responsible journalism and felt pleased with the Welsh media who had doorstepped me that week.

Stealing my face . . . and my voice

On 8 November 2005 – exactly four months to the day that the newspaper had first run a small front-page picture of me injured at Edgware Road – the *Sun* put my face on the cover again. This time my image was huge, covering much of the page, and was headed 'TERROR LAWS'. Beside my bloodied and burnt face there were the words 'Tell Tony He's Right'. The juxtaposition of my face with those words was obvious: this victim of 7/7, representing all the victims, was begging the public to support the Blair government in his House of Commons vote on the new anti-terror laws the following day.

As Ros Coward said in the *Guardian* two days later:

> The implication was clear: this victim had spoken to the *Sun* and was calling on the public to back Blair's tough terror bill, defeated in the Commons last night. The *Sun*'s strong and emotive front page was mentioned several times on other media including BBC Radio 4's *Today* programme and *The World at One*. It was widely recognised as a key element in sending a message to Labour waverers that those whose opinion on the bombings is unimpeachable – the victims – were strongly in favour of the government's hardline stance.

I was out of the country when this happened, trying to get away from media pressure. Ros Coward, however, had previously contacted me, interested in doing a piece on my perceptions as a media academic of the use of victims' images after 7/7. She had done a brief interview with me prior to the *Sun* front page, and so was ready quickly for her *Guardian* piece, 'They Have Given Me Someone Else's Voice – Blair's Voice'. I was happy to read it because it expressed my feelings very fairly.

I believe, as Ros says in the article, that this *Sun* incident is an example of media manipulation, demonstrating the close and causal links between the Murdoch empire and New Labour's leadership. A news empire that has supported the Bush/Blair invasion of Iraq in every single one of its media outlets around the world is, of course, going to emphasise a stereotyped and simplistic notion of the causality of terrorism, and thus push the public to pressurise those Labour Party backsliders opposing Blair's Bill.

Coward's *Guardian* piece quotes me saying, 'It's incredibly ironic that the *Sun*'s rhetoric is as the voice of the people yet they don't actually ask the people involved, the victims what they think. If you want to use my image, the words coming from my mouth would be, "Not in my name Tony". I haven't read anything or seen anything in the past few months to convince me that these laws are necessary.' 'Tell Tony He's Right' is not a comment I would use in any place, time or context, except, of course, on the front page of Rupert Murdoch's *Sun*.

Amusingly, the BBC TV series *Have I Got News For You* picked up the 'Not in my name Tony' comment in its review of the *Sun/Guardian* spat that week, and flashed back to the *Sun* cover to check that these were not the words used. The collision between the two British dailies over the use of my image quickly generated interest from other media, leading up to the end-of-year programmes and articles about 2005. While in Australia in November beginning the writing of this book, I was contacted by almost every British national tabloid and broadsheet, as well as by *Le Monde* and a number of television channels. I kept my head down, because I wanted to write, but knew I would be back in the UK for three weeks in December, just the right time for the 2005 summaries.

I was negotiating directly with a variety of media, as well as through the public relations department at Brunel University, and thought carefully about what priorities I would use in choosing which stories to do. In my three weeks I knew I would need to visit Brunel and discuss with my head of school a possible return to work in January. I would also face my first academic engagement since the bombings, as on 20 December I would be attending an editorial meeting of the international journal *Health, Risk and Society*. I was using up a lot of emotional energy coping with the media flurry around me, and it was this I needed to preserve for the very big step of going back to work, still partially deaf, and regular travel on Tubes and buses.

I decided I had to limit the number of interviews I would give. I would work mainly on stories that were very specific and could be done without a lot of preparation or effort, such as an

Observer piece on friendships that developed out of 7/7. They wanted to focus on Craig and myself as one of the stories and offered us a good restaurant lunch in London to do it. Both my personal and media-related meetings with Craig had gone very well, so I was happy to extend this. I wondered if the recent *Sun* front page would come between us. We enjoyed our lunch, while discussing what aspects we would talk about, since he didn't want to include either his family or politics (which included the *Sun/Guardian* debate) in the interview. Then the *Observer* photographers took their pictures and a good article by William Shaw appeared on 1 January 2006.

Two other media outlets approached me directly with more demanding agendas. They wanted me to extend the political comments I had made in Ros Coward's *Guardian* piece. These were BBC 2's *Newsnight*, as part of its major end-of-year interviews, and BBC Radio 4's *Today*, which was preparing for an end-of-year audience vote on 'Who rules Britain?' with daily items on topics like the economy and the media. I was being positively encouraged to talk about the broader issues around 7 July, which my sons and I had discussed way back in July, and obviously I would take the opportunity. At the same time, I thought about what focus I should adopt for the limited airtime I would get. I needed to consider what kind of programme it was, what its expectations were, and also to try not to repeat my own take on things each time, because I knew that some of the interview questions would repeat themselves. I wanted to reflect on my role as writer as well as victim. This was going to take some thinking and preparation, which would be a good test of how my concussion was progressing, and would give me some clues as to my readiness to go back to work. I was still drawing on the short-term targets strategy that Maggie and Erin had taught me in July.

Another principle in choosing whom to give interviews to was to try to go a bit further with the more personal-style media, as I had distinctly mismanaged the *News of the World* encounter. Murdoch's *Sky News* wanted to do an interview with me that, as the producer emphasised, was not about the kind of politics that the *Sun/Guardian* interaction had exposed. For his end-of-year documentary, he was much more interested in how I now was, and I thought this would mean I could offer him the human interest of my first solo Tube journey from Euston Square Station to Brunel University to see my head of department – the kind of personal touch I had denied the *News of the World* when they wanted to be present at my meeting with the bomb-squad detectives returning my clothes. Most of my contacts with the media since 7/7 had been quite positive, and I wanted to try and do better with the more populist media. With this, as with the more politically oriented encounters, a central interest was how the voices of interviewees as citizens were, or might be, included in a wide variety of media formats and genres.

My interview with Torin Douglas from *Today* as part of the 'Who rules Britain?' series would be quite short. It would be followed by a live studio debate between senior media figures, so I decided that my focus would be around media and power. In the interview as recorded my point was that the interesting question was not whether the media have power (political leaders clearly try to establish good links very early with powerful media owners like Murdoch), but how they use this power and in what forms. I talked briefly about the mainstream media's power to set agendas over how language is used and words are defined, such as we see in the political closure around the word 'terrorism' to exclude the idea of state terrorism from both anti-terror legislation and common media parlance. Without that closure – and in the light of Britain's participation in what many call state-terrorist activities on behalf of political change in Iraq – the British Home Secretary Charles Clarke's definition of support for terrorism – in his framing of the November anti-terror legislation – as anyone who politically encourages violence to bring about change, would have seemed ludicrous. I would then have been interested to talk more about my own research into different newspapers' opening up or closing down of language around the 'war against terror' and the new kinds of warfare in Kosovo and Iraq.

In practice, my cue comments on media power and language were not taken further in interview and then were edited out of what was finally used in the *Today* programme. After a short comment from me on links between political and media leaders, *Today*'s main interest was on the studio professionals, including Greg Dyke (forced out of the BBC for political reasons after the Andrew Gilligan affair) and Piers Morgan (who had to give up editorship of the *Daily Mirror* after acknowledging that the Abu Ghraib-style torture photographs of British soldiers in Iraq he had displayed on the front pages of the paper were fakes). This studio emphasis led to a very stimulating discussion, including Piers' observation that during the Iraq war debacle of endless mistakes by governments, militaries, security agencies and media, it was only media figures like himself and Dyke who had been forced to resign. I thought this was a very valuable debate. My own intention to talk about how their influence differed depending on the openness of a nation's media – in Britain, for example, even politically committed newspapers like the *Daily Mail* and the *Daily Telegraph* print alternative views to their own editorials – was replaced by a much more trenchant point from the mouths of senior media players, who had felt at first hand the realpolitik of media and government power in the UK today.

The *Today* interview went to air on Monday, 12 December, the same morning that my third interview, this time with *Sky News*, was recorded, which indicates how thick and fast they were coming despite my decision to limit the number. In the space of two working days, Friday, 9 December, and Monday,

12 December, two different TV teams, from BBC 2's *Newsnight* and from *Sky News*, recorded me in Janet's sitting room and walked with me to film at Euston Square Station. My plan was always to compare from the inside how these two would work. Here was the academic in me emerging again, because I used as a starting point for my choices of interview the fact that one producer explicitly asked me to talk about politics while the other said he wanted to avoid that. How would these decisions about what I could and couldn't say flow through to inter-viewing style, use of camera and end product? I was perfectly placed, as the interviewee, to see what happened.

It was the *Sky News* producer David Crabtree who did not want political comment from me. This was to be about how I was coping six months on, and would focus on my personal experiences then and now. David knew that I was going that morning to Brunel by Tube for an important meeting about my future at the university, and so he was very accommodating about the length of recording time required. I had suggested beforehand that I was happy to catch first the Circle Line train to Baker Street before changing to my normal Metropolitan Line train to Uxbridge so that they could film me in the same kind of train compartment, sitting if possible in the same seat in the second carriage. This was my first solo journey to work, and my first on the Circle Line, and this would be the *Sky News* item's novelty.

The interview became a very amiable and cooperative meet-ing of the media and the victim/academic. I even suggested one camera shot (showing the board saying, 'Circle Line: 1 min.') that went to air, and David was especially sensitive to the impor-tance of me getting to Brunel on time. Indeed, when the London Underground official (who had to be with us while recording on stations and trains) was delayed, David suggested that they give up on the sequence. For my part, I knew how important the first of seeing me back on the Circle Line was to them. I also knew how long TV production can take, and so had built in more time to spend with them than they thought.

I stepped once more into the second carriage of a Circle Line train, sat on the same side of the carriage next to the double doors as I had on 7 July, and the team travelled two stops with me recording my silent reactions on the way to Baker Street. It was a strange feeling, sitting there again but this time with a camera in my face recording, as TV people love to do, every twitch and shift in my expression. Nonetheless, I trusted them by now, so although I felt exposed I was otherwise comfortable with the experience of getting back on that train. At Baker Street we got off, and the team came with me to the Metropolitan Line platform, where they filmed the sign for the Uxbridge train, as well as a final through-the-window shot of me travelling on to my future at Brunel as the train departed. The victim of 7 July turned seamlessly into the recovering academic.

The *Newsnight* interview was of quite a different order and style. For a start, it took over six hours of my concentrated time. It was exhausting because I was being interviewed and re-interviewed for most of that. The producer suggested, too, a different visual focus, encouraging me as victim and as media academic to talk about images of 7/7 of my choosing. This led to an interesting professional synergy. I was aware as I spoke on camera about the distinct images that I could remember, how I was offering the producer an editing cue. She tightly constructed her theme by editing from these words to shots of me poring over a series of news images. These included the CCTV pictures of the bombers at Luton Station, the iconic images of Davinia Turrell and me at Edgware Road, a family photograph of Jean Charles de Menezes and the photograph I had first seen of Tony Blair receiving the news of the attacks at Gleneagles.

One idea I'd had for the *Newsnight* interview was to begin with that week's Harold Pinter Nobel Prize acceptance speech shown on More4, and then to compare this with a recent article by the former conservative Australian Prime Minister, Malcolm Fraser, in the Melbourne *Age*, who made a number of the same critical points about the Iraq war as Pinter. I wanted to bring attention in this BBC 2 programme to the very wide opposition among public intellectuals in England and Australia to the kind of politics behind Iraq, and to signal my position as part of this broader movement, rather than to speak as an isolated victim. Fraser's words were, of course, more temperate than Pinter's, and his politics are very different. Nevertheless, Fraser called openly in his article for the removal of governments – like Blair's in the UK and Howard's in Australia – which failed the transparency test and made the risks of terrorism greater through their involvement in Iraq. I was careful to quote his exact words: 'We should no longer tolerate governments that claim to do many things to support the war on terror when some things they do help terrorists', as well as his opinion, highly relevant to the recent parliamentary and media debates in both countries about anti-terror legislation, that:

> We should argue for the human rights of those whose views we abhor and despise . . . If we believe that exceptions can be made for terrorists, then we will find pressure to make further exceptions for different groups whose views do not coincide with our own standards. The whole point of the rule of law, the whole point of human rights enshrined in domestic and international law, is that the law applies to all people. Adherence to that principle is the first in the fight against terrorism.

Newsnight recorded this part of the interview early in the six hours, but the producer intervened by saying that she really wanted my views rather than Pinter's or Fraser's. I responded that this was to miss my point, that my views were part of a

broad front, and that in the context of the immediate demoni-
sation of Pinter for his speech that very same week, it was very
important to include Fraser's conservative but parallel discourse.
After some support for my position by the interviewer Liz
McKeen, the producer Shaminder Nahal agreed to a shorter
version. We re-recorded the interview, and I was able to give a
briefer account of my points. The Fraser section was not re-
recorded, on the grounds, Shaminder said, that she would 'try
to get what was needed' from the first attempt that morning.

I was already doubtful that any of what I had to say about
Pinter and Fraser would get to air, and shot off emails later in
the day to various friends and colleagues saying just that. I was
proved right when the programme went out three days later, on
Monday, 12 December.

The *Newsnight* and *Sky News* shows that aired on 12 and 31
December respectively began visually with a similar sense of
terror and urban threat. Both edited their opening shots with
media coverage and reaction to what happened. Sky introduced
the viewer first to an ominously red shot of a Tube tunnel, then
a rapidly edited sequence showing victims on stretchers, emergency support vehicles, police motorbikes, running figures, the
bombed bus, ambulances, helicopters and bandaged, bleeding
survivors emerging from stations. This was overlaid with confused radio reports breaking the news, and was cut with
near-subliminal shots of reflections from the windows of
moving vehicles and shaky mobile-phone pictures taken in the
aftermath. It created a sense of complete disorientation.
Newsnight began with a shot of a newspaper hoarding outside
Euston Square Station announcing that police might be prose-
cuted for the killing of Jean Charles de Menezes. The shot was
disturbed visually by the urgency of cars and silhouetted feet
passing in the foreground, by an ambulance siren that recalled
the day of the attacks, and by the voice-over: 'In the air and on
the street, there is no getting away from 7 July.'

Both items also seemed determined to conclude by portraying me as a resolute victim moving into my future. The last shot of me in the twenty-minute *Sky News* documentary was at Baker Street, with my voice-over saying I was thinking forward. This matched Sky's story of another interviewee, an Underground driver caught in the bombings, who was still receiving counselling and trauma support from London Underground, but is last seen in the documentary driving the train again with another driver. *Newsnight* concluded its seven-minute to-air item with Liz McKeen's voice-over: 'He was against the Iraq war from the start. Five months after the bombing, John Tulloch's opposition to it remains as determined as his battle to regain his health and confidence'.

The focus of *Newsnight* on politics and the effacing of my politics by *Sky News* did lead to some key differences in narrative and visual style. Sky portrayed me and the train driver as near-miss victims quite consistently – the driver had just completed two circuits of the Circle Line and was having a smoke and coffee at Edgware Road station when the bomb went off; the sequences I was in referred to three different near misses (my saying in voice-over as I was seen entering the station how I had just missed my train at Euston Square because of being stopped by a passer-by; sitting in the same seat in the Circle Line train while my voice-over described how I almost pushed myself up to my feet and certain death seconds before the explosion; and recounting from the carriage how shifting my bags at the last minute saved my legs).

While my response to seeing the Sky programme was that it was a tightly controlled and powerfully edited narrative, my first reaction to the seven minutes of interview that made it into *Newsnight* was disappointment, even though I recognised immediately the professionalism of the product. Between recording and seeing the item, I had read an *Observer* piece on the shameful neglect of Harold Pinter's Nobel speech right across the

British media, and their dropping everything I had said in inter-view about him seemed to me another example. However, a couple of weeks later I ran the tape of the programme to my family in Australia, and they liked it a lot. Rowan, for instance, commented that this kind of treatment was unlikely to be screened in Australia, and that if I had got in my points about Pinter and Fraser I could have been accused of having prepared and pre-rehearsed my position – the very accusation I was making about Tony Blair in the part that did go to air. We talked over the interview in some detail, and I learned from that dis-cussion a lot about the quality of professionalism in *Newsnight*'s team.

What was it that made the item so powerful? Our collective impression was that the interview combined a number of modes of address which are usually kept separate in mainstream media. It opened with a politicising urgency conveyed by the newspaper hoarding outside Euston Square Station. Of the killing of Jean Charles de Menezes, it read: 'Tube Shooting. Police May Face Charges'.

The urgency of this sequence – the frontal shots of the sta-tion obscured by heavy moving traffic, the hoarding sliced continually by the black, silhouetted legs of pedestrians – was immediately followed by a slower shot in deeper space as the station was opened up by the camera and Liz and I were fol-lowed without edits around the turn in the stairs down towards the ticket office. Liz's voice-over continued the theme by saying I was returning to my starting point on the Tube that day I sat so close to Mohammad Sidique Khan. The sympathetic tone of her voice and my slow pace down the stairs encouraged viewers to identify with me, the victim. This was supported by a close-up of my face as I recalled the explosion that day.

My words cued the signature for the entire item and an extended sequence followed of me sitting at Janet's dining table with the images from the attacks: in my hospital bed greeting

Prince Charles; CCTV footage of the four suicide bombers at Luton Station accompanied by personalised comments from me about my movements and those of the bombers that morning; and then, with a more academic commentary from me about it, the picture of Davinia Turrell and Paul Dadge.

This shift from me being a victim to a more distanced academic was important because it offered me the programme's authority to talk about the next image, the photograph of Tony Blair at Gleneagles. I was, I said in close-up, in pain when I first saw that picture, but any suggestion that this might have caused me to be unfair or highly subjective in my judgement of Blair was undercut by the way the *Newsnight* item had established my role earlier as an academic, and would again later by showing me commenting 'professionally' about images. It was also undercut by the sequence's final judgement that I had long opposed the Iraq war and that none of the horrible cruelties of the bombings had changed that view.

Liz, visually and audibly a sympathetic on-screen interviewer, fed me the *Sun/Guardian* story, which had been the focus of Jeremy Paxman's introduction. She gave me the opportunity to talk as an academic about the shift of different iconic images between July and November 2005. Liz also asked about my anger with political leaders rather than with the bombers themselves. I responded: 'The anger is with the people who manipulated us, people who had decided to go to war six months before, as government Whitehall documents have revealed. Those people, and of course the people behind the young men who carried out the bombing.'

Throughout this, the screen was dominated by images from the media, and by the interviewer and interviewee in tight one- or two-shots. Comments about the bombers not being simply 'other' (with me pointing to the picture of Mohammad Sidique Khan as a teacher's assistant listening to his colleagues and to his young pupils) were interwoven with my personalised, shocked expressivity in close-up at 'How could they?' do the terrible things of 7 July.

My professional academic life was seen by *Newsnight*, and by *Sky News*, too, to depend on how I would respond to travelling on Tube trains again. On *Newsnight* my future was seen to be made harder by my recognition, as I gestured with a hand at the lack of any further security at Euston Square Station, that it could all happen again – a comment more with the British government in mind than my own ability, psychologically and physically, to get back on that train.

On *Newsnight* the station shots acted as bookends to a layered personal, political and professional academic account, which in its finale took us back to the frenetic pace of a frightened, damaged London at Edgware Road on 7 July. Now, though, there was a strong, sympathetic voice-over blending all the layers into a new determination: my political opposition to the Iraq war remained as strong as my battle to regain health and confidence. This, as I'm sure the producer would agree, made this more persuasive TV.

In contrast the *Sky News* documentary was a well-edited narrative telling a single, supposedly non-political tale via different personal memories – narrated by a train driver and by a victim at Edgware Road, by a fireman at King's Cross and by a doctor at Tavistock Square – of horror and of London's resistance to terror. The editing together of images and sounds was impressively controlled, both within and between sequences. While *Newsnight* used my words that I recalled the explosion and its aftermath as a series of separate images to cue the strategy of me talking about the media's coverage throughout, *Sky News* used colour matches, shaking hand-held images and voice-overs to tell a shocking but unified tale.

The sequence leading up to the explosion began with the words of the train driver and the fireman: 'It was just an ordinary day'; 'It was a day like any other.' The fireman's ordinary day is quickly seen to be changing. He talks about watching *Sky News* with his mates at 9.20 a.m., and hearing of a power surge at Edgware Road. We see the men leave frame, the empty room resonating powerfully with the blue flashing light from their vehicle. This image bleeds into an extreme close-up of the fire engine's blue light matched to the rhythm of a soft, pulsing music score and the fireman's voice can be heard saying, 'Edgware Road'. The picture fades to black – a regular editing motif of this documentary which suggested, I think, both passing time and the darkness of events – and then immediately takes us back, still with its pulsing music, into that frightening red shot of the tunnel at Edgware Road. This time, though, we see an extreme close-up of train windows moving slowly and relentlessly left to right, and then the back of the Circle Line train as it disappears ominously around the bend of that red tunnel, and we hear my voice saying how just as it entered the tunnel I began to get up. The next visual shows me sitting alert in the train, making a decision not to move into the double doorway where the suicide bomber is – one of my near misses. Then we see more dark tunnel, and a train flashing by in the opposite direction, before my next words, the climax of the sequence: 'And the next second, the explosion happened.' These are edited over another colour-reduced but yellow-saturated mobile-phone image of the carriage.

The programme then cuts to a close-up of the polystyrene coffee cup of the train driver being stirred as his voice-over says, 'There was an almighty thump and the room shook.' We see him running down the station stairs and realising it was a bomb. Then a cut to shaky, blurred mobile-phone camera close-ups of shattered train windows, confused human shapes and yellow colours brought back my story, as my voice-over says, 'There's a yellow colour, not exactly like a sudden flash – everything goes yellow, a horrible yellow colour. Everything's pulled and stretched. I don't see debris. I don't see bodies flying about. I just see everything wrenched and stretched and pulled.'

The power and novelty of the editing here is in its use of colour and a shaking camera to match what I was saying about the yellow-toned stretching and wrenching of my carriage by the explosion. The train driver speaks of his disbelief as, over a close-up of his staring eyes, he says, 'It was just complete carnage. Even from this view, you could see the sides of the train were sticking out from the bomb blast, there were bits of the train all over the place, and of course there was the first body I saw that was lying outside the train.'

These sequences took just two minutes and twenty-three seconds. What followed was of the same quality: a driving narrative, intelligently controlled in a series of simultaneous and sequential matching edits and overlaps of colour, vox pop witness stories and sounds, which tell Sky's story of horror down below ground in London on that ordinary day.

Sky News had one other important story. There were some politics in this documentary after all, since the first half ended by showing the solidarity with the victimised British people of the politicians Blair, Bush and Chirac at Gleneagles; and the second half concluded with London's mayor Ken Livingstone speaking, juxtaposed with the two-minute silence at Trafalgar Square. Unlike the *Newsnight* image of Blair, static and chosen by me for discussion, *Sky News* had a seriously statesmanlike Blair, speaking directly to the TV camera about Britain's unassailable unity. Similarly, the image of Livingstone shows him speaking about London as a great multicultural city, which is reinforced as his words are heard while the camera roams around the crowds at King's Cross on 7 July and during the two minutes' silence at Trafalgar Square, resting occasionally on faces from all over the world and on the banners of Muslims horrified by the attack. The penultimate image is of a young black man in sunglasses looking forward resolutely to camera, and is followed by the unfurling of a Union Jack bearing the words 'We are not afraid'. Ken Livingstone says in voice-over, 'The City of London is the greatest in the world because everybody lives side by side in harmony, and London will not be divided by this cowardly attack. They will stand together in solidarity around those who have been injured, those who have been bereaved. And that is why I'm proud to be mayor of this city.'

The politically discerning viewer might notice some differences between Blair's and Livingstone's words about unity. For Blair, as the camera pulls out to reveal an international array of premiers and presidents, the unity is among leaders of nations:

> All our countries have suffered from the impact of terrorism . . . We are united in our resolve to confront and defeat this terrorism which is not an attack on one nation but on all nations and civilised people everywhere.

But for Livingstone:

> This was not a terrorist attack against the mighty and the powerful. It was not aimed at presidents and prime ministers. It was aimed at ordinary working-class people, black and white, Muslim and Christian, Hindu and Jew, young and old.

The old 'Red Ken', as the *Sun* still calls him, was here debating with the New Labour and neo-con leaders at Gleneagles, as well as condemning the terrorists. The politics of dissent was maybe just glimpsed in this documentary. However, overall, there are no critics in the Sky item, only consensus on the unity of a multicultural Britain. Even though we hear about the train driver's fears of another bombing and about the killing of Jean Charles de Menezes, Sir Ian Blair is introduced to tell us that the shoot-to-kill policy is necessary, and the documentary moves quickly on from the terrible mistake and tragedy of the killing to more footage of me dealing with my trauma on the Tube.

The ending of *Year in Review 2005 –Terror* is nationalistically symbolic and politically resolute. Blair's earlier words are powerfully reinforced by a people ethnically diverse but as united and positive about their city as the Londoners we meet in the next chapter, in Ian McEwan's novel *Saturday*.

TEN

Another Day

I didn't attend the 7/7 memorial at St Paul's Cathedral in November. Instead I was abroad reading a novel. I knew there would be more pressure then from the media, which I wanted to avoid. I was also responding to playwright Phyllis Nagy's comments at Chichester about how people use memorial services to close off feelings of guilt. Friends were talking to me about it being some kind of closure if I were to go to the service, but that wasn't the way my emotions were going. In any case, I wasn't looking for closure from the government by way of a formal state-funded service.

In fact from the time of the killing of Jean Charles de Menezes I had been aware that what I wanted was the opposite, an opening out of debate. I had rung the bomb squad that morning of the shooting obsessed with my report for a Ph.D. examination. After I heard the terrible story of his killing, I scrutinised newspaper after newspaper to find out what happened and why.

Now, again, in early November, I wanted to search for people speaking in public spaces, with different or alternative views – not only to Blair's but to my own as well. So I went abroad for a few days in late October and read a novel about another day of violence and guilt and trauma, Ian McEwan's *Saturday*.

I'd heard about the novel already. I knew it began with what seems to be a terrorist attack, a plane burning low over a part of London I'd been living close to since the bombings, and where one of the abortive attacks took place on 21 July. I knew that McEwan focused the novel around the anti-Iraq war march in London, and that he didn't agree with the protest wholeheartedly. I knew, too, from reviews that the book was an attempt to describe happiness and guilt in everyday life in the post-9/11 Western world – I wanted to explore both of those. I wanted to see what questions McEwan asked about it all, and how he developed a fictional response.

As with my exploration of the different ways that theatre and TV approached the attacks, Iraq and the 'war against terror', I wanted to experience a different kind of vision from my own as a sociologist. In this case, a novel.

McEwan had not been able to ply his trade immediately after 9/11. To Jeffrey Brown of Online NewsHour, he said on 13 April 2005:

> I couldn't think about novels at all. It seemed the only writing that was appropriate to that horrendous event was journalism, reportage . . . And, in fact, this is a novel that is set not about that event, but its shadow, and it casts a very long shadow, not only over international affairs, but in the very small print of our lives.

It was precisely this that I was dealing with after 7/7. The terrible attacks, the huge event, had affected my life personally, and in a much wider way, too. The novel begins, 'Some hours before dawn Henry Perowne, a neurosurgeon, wakes to find himself already in motion, pushing back the covers from a sitting position, and then rising to his feet.' That grabbed my attention immediately, because the character's sleeplessness was the same as I had been experiencing regularly, almost every night since the blast.

In these first pages of the novel there is a motif of sleeplessness and an atmosphere of terror. Waking in the pre-dawn summer and autumn in a part of London twice attacked by terrorists in July, I had often faced that combination. I wondered what McEwan would do, now that he had discovered his post-9/11 writing voice, with that time in the night when Henry, like me, found himself in temporary isolation and introspection.

He looks out at London, feeling a 'sustained, distorting euphoria. Perhaps down at the molecular level there's been a chemical accident while he slept – something like a spilled tray of drinks, prompting dopamine-like receptors to initiate a kindly cascade of intra-cellular events'. He looks across the affluent Georgian square (from the house where McEwan himself lives) towards Charlotte Street and out over Ken Livingstone's – and *Sky News'* – multicultural London. Henry thinks the city is 'a success, a brilliant invention, a biological masterpiece – millions teeming around the accumulated and layered achievements of the centuries, as though around a coral reef, entertaining themselves, harmonious for the most part, nearly everyone wanting it to work'.

As he continues to look out of his open window on that cold early morning in February 2003, two events which provide the thematic structure for the novel are introduced. The first is his relationship through books with his daughter Daisy:

> For some years now she's been addressing what she believes is his astounding ignorance, guiding his literary education, scolding him for poor taste and insensitivity . . . for fifteen years he barely touched a non-medical book at all . . . Still, he submits to her reading lists – they're his means of remaining in touch as she grows away from her family into unknowable

womanhood in a suburb in Paris; tonight she'll be home for
the first time in six months – another cause for euphoria.

McEwan is always strong on our struggle to make a disinte-
grating world mean something. Sometimes (as with Henry and
Daisy) it is somewhere caught between scientific and artistic viewpoints; and McEwan's particular historical angst is often worked
through personal violence. Here, at the novel's start, Henry has
been reading Darwin, but he has also been listening to the radio,
and mention of Hans Blix addressing the UN situates the historical moment. We know we are on the edge of the Iraq war.

The Blix reference also introduces the second event of
Henry's sleepless morning: the burning plane over London,
which he takes to be a terrorist attack. It is not, though the
media think to begin with that it is. They mention fearfully that
the pilot is a Chechen and there is Islamic literature in the cock-
pit. Henry becomes obsessed with media accounts of these
'terrorists'. It becomes almost his personal story, his night-time
discovery of a culture of fear that threatens him and his sense of
safety: in his house, and in London.

The threat to London is then realised in the novel by a different kind of violence. On the Saturday evening, there is a
horrific invasion of Henry's home by two very violent men he
encountered earlier in the day after a minor car accident. He
had not managed the confrontation well, particularly with the
pathologically violent Baxter, whom he had talked out of giving
him a beating. Henry, quick with words and professional discipline, had spotted and described to Baxter his probably fatal
and certainly totally debilitating condition, Huntington's
Disease, before escaping to his Saturday squash game.

On one hand, McEwan draws Baxter's meaningless end inti-
mately into the sadness of many of our lives via Henry's
touching relationship with his mother – a dementia patient as
was my own mother – whom he visits ritually, then guiltily leaves

behind with carers. On the other hand, in a wider way, Baxter's violence operates in the novel as a mood-parallel to the violence of terrorism and the Iraq war.

This is Saturday, 15 February 2003, the day of the massive anti-war demonstration in London. Indeed, it was while Henry was trying to avoid the blocked roads around Tottenham Court Road that he had his accident with Baxter. In his kitchen that evening, before Baxter's invasion of the house, Daisy, who has just published her first book of poetry, talks with Henry about Iraq:

> 'You're saying we're invading Iraq because we haven't got a choice. I'm amazed at the crap you talk, Dad. You know very well these extremists, the Neo-cons, have taken over America. Cheney, Rumsfeld, Wolfowitz. Iraq was always their pet project. Nine-eleven was their big chance to talk Bush round . . . But there's nothing linking Iraq to nine-eleven, or to Al-Qaeda generally, and no really scary evidence of WMD. Didn't you hear Blix yesterday? And doesn't it ever occur to you that in attacking Iraq we're doing the very thing the New York bombers wanted us to do – lash out, make more enemies in Arab countries and radicalise Islam. Not only that, we're getting rid of their old enemy, the godless Stalinist tyrant.'
>
> 'And I suppose they wanted us to destroy their training camps and drive the Taliban out of Afghanistan, and force Bin Laden on the run, and have their financial networks disrupted and had their key guys locked up . . .'
>
> She cuts in and her voice is loud. 'Stop twisting my words. No one's against going after al-Qaeda. We're talking about Iraq. Why is it that the few people I've met who aren't against this crappy war are all over forty? What is it about getting old? Can't get close to death soon enough?'

Henry, drinking heavily, responds with his own, rather bitter rebuke to her generation:

'The genocide and torture, the mass graves, the security apparatus, the criminal totalitarian state – the iPod generation doesn't want to know. Let nothing come between them and their ecstasy clubbing and cheap flights and reality TV . . . You think you're all lovely and gentle and blameless, but the religious nazis loathe you. What do you think the Bali bombing was about? The clubbers clubbed. Radical Islam hates your freedom.'

She mimes being taken aback. 'Dad, I'm sorry you're so sensitive about your age. But Bali was Al-Qaeda, not Saddam. Nothing you've just said justifies invading Iraq.'

Henry, well into his third glass of champagne, tries another argument. Since Daisy is a published writer, doesn't she care about her 'fellow writers in Arab jails, in the very region where writing was invented'?

'Oh for God's sake, not that relativist stuff again. And you keep drifting off the point. No one wants Arab writers in jail. But invading Iraq isn't going to get them out.'

'It might. Here's a chance to turn one country around. Plant a seed. See if it flourishes and spreads.'

'You don't plant seeds with cruise missiles. They're going to hate the invaders. The religious extremists will get stronger. There'll be less freedom, more writers in prison.'

'My fifty pounds says three months after the invasion there'll be a free press in Iraq, and unmonitored Internet access too. The reformers in Iran will be encouraged, those Syrian and Saudi and Libyan potentates will be getting the jitters.'

Daisy says, 'Fine. And my fifty says it'll be a mess and even you will wish it never happened.'

On they go into the evening gathering of Henry, Daisy, Henry's newspaper lawyer wife Rosalind, his late-teenage son

Theo, who is a British blues musician about to make it big, and John Grammaticus, the famous poet, father of Rosalind. Daisy has brought her new book of poetry, *My Saucy Bark*, to present to Grammaticus, to end a jealous separation between them.

The quarrels of everyday life, between Grammaticus and Daisy over poetry, and between Henry and both his children over the Iraq war, are suddenly interrupted. Baxter and his underclass accomplice Nigel force their way in, smash Grammaticus' nose, and threaten to slit Rosalind's throat, ordering Daisy to strip off her clothes. However, something unexpected happens as the men get ready to rape her. At Grammaticus' prompt, Daisy begins reciting poetry, though neither Henry nor Baxter is literary enough to know that it is not her own work but Matthew Arnold's *Dover Beach*.

Impatient with this poetic intervention, Nigel says to Baxter, 'I'll take the knife while you do the business.' Baxter, though, has moved into one of his dangerously mobile, illness-induced moods: 'Baxter appears suddenly elated . . . and is saying excitedly, "You wrote that. You *wrote that*".' The invasion now ends quickly. Baxter wants Daisy's book, and more chance of life. Henry has lied to him to lure him away from Daisy, that he has a research publication on trials for a cure for Huntington's upstairs in his study. Baxter follows the fearful Henry up the stairs. Nigel, disgusted for the second time that day by Baxter's weakness, slams his way out of the house. Theo runs to his father's aid, and in a brief fight father and son hurl Baxter down the stairs. It is an overt moment of social guilt in the novel:

> Baxter is . . . looking directly at Henry with an expression, not so much of terror, as dismay. And Henry sees in the wide brown eyes a sorrowful accusation of betrayal. He, Henry Perowne, possesses so much – the work, the money, status, the home, above all the family . . . and he has done nothing,

given nothing to Baxter who has so little that is not wrecked
by his defective gene, and who is soon to have even less.

But Henry does give Baxter something: he operates on him
successfully that same evening. Afterwards, Henry thinks about
the pleasure and control he gets from cutting into people:

> For the past two hours he's been in a dream of absorption
> that has dissolved all sense of time, and all awareness of the
> other parts of his life . . . This state of mind brings a con-
> tentment he never finds with any passive form of
> entertainment. Books, cinema, even music can't bring him to
> this . . . This benevolent dissociation seems to require diffi-
> culty, prolonged demands on concentration and skills,
> pressure, problems to be solved, even danger . . . he's happier
> than at any other point of his day off, his valuable Saturday.

So, while for millions of others the high point of that Saturday
is the anti-war demonstration, for Henry it is operating on
Baxter. But Henry's surgical skill, which he calls his 'qualification
to exist', is not the only reason he saves Baxter that night. The
end of the book finds him where he was at the beginning, alone
in the pre-dawn, looking out again from his open bedroom
window. He ponders now the contrast: not only between his life
and Baxter's, but between the drunks and junkies of the night
and the multicultural crowds of working people who come there
at lunchtime, when the gates of the gardens are opened up.
Those in the day are mixed in background, positive in outlook,
fit from gyms and unoppressed. At night the people share the
dim fate of being unemployable, alcoholic or, like Baxter, unable
to 'remember today what he resolved to do yesterday. No
amount of social justice will cure or disperse this enfeebled army
haunting the public places of the town. So what then?'

No social theorist, Henry thinks beyond Baxter to his mother:

'She's not dead,' Henry kept telling himself. But her life, all lives, seemed tenuous when he saw how quickly, with what ease, all the trappings, all the fine details of a lifetime could be packed and scattered, or junked.'

This is a major novelist at work on what de Zengotita also contrasts: life and guilt, the virtuality of our everyday lives and the nothingness of life at ground zero, the reality of life faced with death. Henry thinks about the 'details of a lifetime' in face of the meaninglessness of ageing and death. He imagines a middle-aged doctor standing at this same window a hundred years ago in his silk dressing gown two hours before dawn, believing in progress: 'You might envy this Edwardian gent all he didn't know. If he had young boys, he would lose them within a dozen years, at the Somme. And what was their body count, Hitler, Stalin, Mao? Fifty million, a hundred? If you described the hell that lay ahead, if you warned him, the good doctor – an affable product of prosperity and decades of peace – would not believe you. Beware the utopianists, zealous men certain of the path to the ideal social order.'

Here we see McEwan the narrator of horrendous events (post-Auschwitz, post-gulag, post-9/11) together with McEwan the teller of domestic details, faced with another kind of ground zero at the end of our lives. He warns us of a reality working at both those levels – internationally and personally – shattering the mirrors before which we all perform.

McEwan is more comfortable at the personal level, and a number of his reviewers point to the meeting of Henry and his mother as among the best writing in the novel. Henry is, in his own way, a utopianist, with 'one small fixed point of conviction'. He has temporarily saved the life of a man who might have killed them all after publicly raping his daughter. He is now determined to persuade his family and the police to drop charges against Baxter. He wonders whether this is seeking for-giveness for his guilt of affluence, or whether it is the impact of age 'when the remaining years take on their finite aspect, and you begin to feel for yourself the first chill, you watch a dying man with a closer, more brotherly interest'. He prefers 'to believe that it's realism: they'll all be diminished by whipping a man on his way to hell.'

Henry recalls the poem that Daisy recited which affected Baxter so much. As a doctor he rationalises this by thinking that perhaps any poem would have cued the sudden mood change of a fatally sick man. Yet he is not quite convinced by that scientific explanation, and pines for something the criminal has that he hasn't. Baxter, he remembers, was transfixed by the magic of Daisy's art and 'was reminded how much he wanted to live. No one can forgive him the use of the knife. But Baxter heard what Henry never has, and probably never will.'

Of course both these men use the knife, but somehow Baxter seems to have more; and Henry, even after returning at the end of the novel to the sexual scent and cosy warmth of Rosalind in bed, is deeply disturbed as he looks out of his window again. The future of London, beyond his windows, lies as vulnerable as at the beginning. London, like Baxter alone in his hospital room, faces awful ravages ahead:

> London, his small part of it, lies wide open, impossible to defend, waiting for its bomb, like a hundred other cities. Rush hour will be a convenient time. It might resemble the Paddington crash – twisted rails, buckled, upraised commuter coaches, stretchers handed out through broken windows, the hospital's Emergency Plan in action . . . The authorities agree, an attack's inevitable . . . But from the top of his day, this is a future that's harder to read, a horizon indistinct with possibilities.

McEwan wrote these words before 7/7, and on that Thursday in July I did encounter at the terrorists' 'convenient time' of rush hour the buckled commuter coaches. I was subject to the Emergency Plan in action at the same hospital that had dealt with the Paddington train crash. I am not, though, making a point about the author's powers of foresight in *Saturday*, so much as about his obsession with weaving his prediction through the novel.

The obsession of *Saturday* lies in its mood: the culture of fear is everywhere. But there is something else in the dialogue, acting in counterpoint to the mood, which made it particularly powerful for me. On the surface, there was so much that played with my own experience, even that clarifying adrenalin rush Henry has at the beginning. It seemed to me as I finished the book in early November that the somewhat utopian ending, as well as the love and mutual tutoring between Henry and Daisy, suggests that in asking his questions about hope and guilt, mutual love and distrust, affluence (his own, my own) and the violence of poverty, McEwan's novel is also asking questions about the clichés of innocence – whether Henry's and Daisy's position as innocent victims of Baxter and Nigel, or my own construction by the media as innocent victim of the suicide bombers. In *Saturday* 'innocent victim' is neither seen as an acceptable status nor a social truth in the face of terror and disintegration.

McEwan asks questions without giving answers, and through them *Saturday* offers us the pleasures of what Joanna Bourke calls a new civic engagement, written out of the very heart of the mood of fear. This is, I think, because *Saturday* is a strongly dialogic novel: of voices in debate, and humans caught between the dialogue of fierce competition and introspective togetherness. McEwan himself was not an anti-war marcher, hating the certainty of voices on either side. Some of his better reviewers capture well this Iraq dialogue in *Saturday*. Lewis Jones wrote in the *Daily Telegraph*:

> The impending war lurks in the background, and sometimes looms in close-up. Perowne is ambivalent towards it – a hawk to his doveish children, a dove to a hawkish American

colleague. On the one hand he has an Iraqi patient who has been tortured by Saddam's regime and he deplores the smug slogan 'Not in my name'. On the other he is concerned that an invasion might be disastrous, and he does not quite trust Tony Blair.

Saturday, as Lee Siegel wrote in the *Nation*, is a deliberately ambiguous novel about 'consciousness that illuminates the sources of politics'. Politics in *Saturday* is represented by Tony Blair, in a telling moment when he enters a high profile reception at Tate Modern and congratulates Henry on his work. Henry is momentarily flattered, until Blair says he has two of his works hanging on the wall at No. 10, and refuses to concede that Henry is not a famous painter. It is not only a moment of systematic lying that comes from an experience McEwan himself had with Blair, but also a moment of refusal to listen, debate and discuss. *The Times* reviewer Jasper Gerard captures this moment of a politician performing in front of mirrors:

> McEwan corrected him, but Blair still insisted that he had McEwans on his walls: proof that nobody does sincerity as convincingly as Blair, because his lies deceive even himself. In *Saturday*, set on the day of London's anti-Iraq war march, McEwan uses the insight to weigh up the prime minister's truthfulness; the neurosurgeon watches Blair on television spelling out his case for war. There is no discernible doubt.

No discernible doubt in the performance of politics; yet the novel spoke to me very directly about alternative voices of public debate, about terror and recurrent violence (I had been violently mugged in Madrid only three years before facing the suicide bomber at Edgware Road), about Iraq and about multicultural London, about care and guilt over infirmity in one's family, and about ageing and that new, precarious sense I have after 7/7 of the finite years that lie ahead. It debated history, realism and relativism, and the discussion of these things in my own academic profession.

As a professional sociologist I agreed with the review by Lynn Wells of *Saturday*, that McEwan poses 'the very real problems facing British society, domestic and international, acted out in the conflict between Perowne and Baxter', only to efface these at the end in an 'imperialist fantasy of middle-class dominance', crowned by a poem about Dover:

> With London's bomb inevitably coming, one gets no sense of a need for urgent cultural change from the novel's ending, which papers over the implications of the disparity between the doctor and the street-thug and suggests that life can go on happily for the English middle class.

However, that is a sociological reading, and I think reduces something which is of quite another order in the novel. It is a fiction which speaks a different kind of dialogue. The review misses the powerful connection between terrorism and McEwan's 'enfeebled army' conveyed not in the sociology but the mood of the novel. And it misses the emotional honesty of *Saturday*'s dialogue, as in Henry and Daisy's discussion about Iraq.

While I disagree with McEwan's stance on the Iraq war, I like the way he writes his fiction about it, the collision of violence very close to us and far away from us, and above all his openness in talking – as Martin Crimp does in his different way in *Cruel and Tender* – about the potential terrorist in all of us. Henry, who as we've seen hurls Baxter down the stairs and later operates on him while drunk, is no more innocent than the 'bad guy' himself.

Saturday's structure and form are as tight from first scene to last (with another aeroplane flying over Henry at the end) as the competitive squash game the surgeon plays against his American anaesthetist. However, unlike in the game, there is no winner, only a determination by McEwan to raise questions about the neo-cons and Blair, the underclass and terrorists, the evils of the Saddam regime, and the ways in which these interweave with our daily lives. These obsessions permeate what we say to each other, and how we act together. In particular, *Saturday* asks us to enter the minds of the violent – but in dialogue not in fear.

I felt I had probably been better served reading a fictional work than going to the memorial service for the dead and injured of my Thursday, which was in one way another opportunity to represent Britain standing unbowed against evil. *Saturday* was about another day, in February 2003, not in July 2005, and it resonated with its own dialogue, different from the prevailing questions in the press about finding the 'bad guys' immediately after 7/7. However, McEwan's questions – about terror and violence, guilt and betrayal, opportunity and oppression, power and weakness, having a voice and being voiceless, culture and civilisation, multiculturalism and the underclass, gender and age, rhetoric and action, seeking an ambivalent truth and telling self-serving lies – are equally relevant to those we should ask about 9/11 and 7/7. We need another novel like *Saturday*, but placed elsewhere – maybe in Beeston – where not Henry, but Mohammad and Shehzad are the subjects. I wonder whether we have a novelist so bold?

My point in talking about *Saturday*, and *5/11*, and *Newsnight* is that in Britain we have, in addition to the enormously positive force of working professional people – who helped me so much on and after 7/7 – an ambivalent or alienated force of public intellectuals and communicators who are desperately keen to find a different way of being democratic to that increasingly being imposed upon us, as well as on the people of Iraq. The journalists, novelists and playwrights I have talked about come from different shades of political opinion. At their best, they are ambivalent and uncertain about Iraq, terrorism and violence. However, they have seen very clearly the illegal war, the political mess and the spin of our politicians and their media friends. Many would subscribe to George Orwell's view that, 'Political language . . . is designed to make lies sound truthful and murder respectable, and to give an appearance of solidity to pure wind.'

In the first few months after 7 July, I began to read and engage with this group of people who were focusing on Iraq. I felt in their writings a strong sense of an alternative democracy, of civic engagement. Even as disillusionment is spreading among many friends and colleagues powerless in the face of the guilt and responsibility they feel for the Iraq war, this engagement is spreading in our media and cultural life. This is happening not just in the newspapers, novels and plays that I have described, but in areas I haven't had the space to discuss.

One of these, a review by John Berger of a Paris retrospective of Francis Bacon's paintings, was very much in my mind as I reconsidered my opinion of the *Newsnight* interview. In the Iraq war year of 2003, Berger found in Bacon's half-century-old art our current world of Fallujah and 'collateral damage': 'What is different in Bacon's vision is that there are no witnesses and there is no grief. Nobody painted by him notices what is happening to somebody else painted by him. Such ubiquitous indifference is crueller than any mutilation.' And yet Berger concludes his review positively, as I want to end this book, in pointing to an alternative way of speaking:

> On the side of the powerful there is a conformism of fear . . . and the mouthing of words that no longer mean anything. Such muteness is what Bacon painted. On the other side there are multitudinous, disparate, sometimes disappearing, languages with whose vocabularies a sense can be made of life even if, particularly if, that sense is tragic.

Berger's words remind me why I began to respect the producers of *Newsnight* for editing out my thoughts about Pinter and Fraser. What they created instead was a form that mixed the different voices and TV styles of personal interview, academic analysis and political comment. Their editing left me a little more ambiguous, puzzling over, as much as observing, what was on the screen. The programme stimulated me to ask questions rather than to find answers in it for the problems of terrorism and Iraq. As Berger says, these are the questions that make up the disparate, sometimes disappearing languages whose words allow some sense to be made of our lives.

This is not to say that *Newsnight* was not itself contrived; part of the reason that I spent time talking about it earlier was to make this clear. In my reading, the producers did me a favour by not making me seem prepared and rehearsed, as I felt Blair had been at Gleneagles. However, the risk to democracy is not that all narratives are performative, whether the performance is that of *Newsnight* or of Pinter in his Nobel Prize speech, or of New Labour's intensive narrative about the context of the terror attacks. The risk is that we only get to see one version of a narrative, and have that presented publicly via the monologue of spin as the truth. That is why I complained in the *Guardian* about the *Sun* stealing my voice (and my graphically injured face) for Tony Blair's anti-terror legislation. That is why Pinter in his Nobel speech speaks of there being no hard distinctions 'between what is true and what is false' in drama. That is why McEwan presents his central dialogue between Henry and Daisy in *Saturday*, where tellingly he presents views both about the international ambitions of the US neo-cons and the tortured Iraqi surgeon for whom McEwan believes the war is being fought.

A major novelist like McEwan chooses to play this dialogue through the intensely localised environment of one household in one city on one day. A significant theatre festival like

Chichester may perform its dialogue through a number of plays debating in different ways the spin and trickery in our politics, art and everyday lives. A quality television production like *Newsnight* may juggle in new ways entirely conventional discourses and forms. A newspaper art critic can rediscover a new relevance for a painter whose major works have long shouted soundlessly at their publics. My point is that across a very broad front of TV, newspapers, theatre, literature and fine arts, public intellectuals have exposed themselves – as well as the forms they work within – to the discipline of asking questions about Iraq and freedom. It is time we asked no less of our politicians.

Another, Better Day

Mohammad Sidique Khan,

On 7 July 2005 you tried to kill me. You personally killed six others in my carriage, and your accomplice 'soldiers' killed many more.

I recall three images of you regularly to my mind, and two of these are before me as I write. One is only in my memory, because despite my uncertainty about it when I gave the police my report of the explosion you caused, I am now fairly certain that we looked at each other across the second carriage of that Circle Line train. My memory tells me that there was another man sitting with you and that you both looked across to me, but maybe it plays me false.

What I do know is that when we stared at each other briefly, we meant nothing to each other, both part of the detritus of time, space and the distancing, unfriendly business of everyday life. Except that you had made a decision to change that, and even as you looked across at me you were probably thinking not about me but – because they say you were the leader of your group – about what the other bombers were doing. We were just your targets, about to 'taste the reality' of the appalling things being done by various governments to people in the Islamic world.

A second image of you, which I have now before me, is one I found on the cover of the *Sun* newspaper on 14 July 2005. It is a photograph of you working in a classroom as a teacher's assistant at Hillside Primary School, with a teacher on your right, and a pixelated image, perhaps of one of your pupils, in the foreground. You are looking to your left out of frame, listening, contemplative, with a pencil clasped in your hand. Other teachers from the school, reported in the *Sun*, described you as 'gently spoken, endlessly patient and hugely popular with children'. The image I am looking at supports your colleagues' view.

What you are thinking about is probably a new version of an old story, which you described to the *Times Educational Supplement* in April 2002. In the image I suspect you are thinking once again about the problems of vulnerability, backwardness, poverty and the too-fast turnover of pupils in your school. Bad as it was, you felt that your school was the best in the area although you complained in the *TES* that it would take years to improve through government regeneration funds.

As you wrote your notes with that pencil, were you slotting your current thoughts into the ingrained tactics and resources you employed as a well-loved mentor to underprivileged children and their parents? Your role at the school, which served the children of the poorest families living in cheap, short-term rental properties in Leeds, was crucial. With more than a 50 per cent turnover of these children in two terms, you were appointed as one of two learning mentors to liaise with the pupils' previous schools to find records and assess their maths and literacy when they arrived. Everybody said you were very good at that. There is a lot of thought behind your eyes in this photograph; and in the *TES* interview you had told us about your pride in your job and your frustration with the unfairness within your community. And the word is still strong in Beeston, as I write, of what you did in the community to help kids against drugs and prostitution.

The third image is from a website, and is part of the al-Jazeera video broadcast on 1 September 2005. Again you have a pencil or pen in your hand. But now you are holding it in declamatory mode, thrusting downwards beneath your red chequered keffiyeh as you eyeball us, talking the talk of a soldier straight to camera:

> I'm going to keep this short and to the point because it's all been said before by far more eloquent people than me. And our words have no impact upon you, therefore I'm going to talk to you in a language that you understand. Our words are dead until we give them life with our blood.

In my second image, you were listening. However, in this third image you are talking, in the Yorkshire accent that shocked many British people: 'Your democratically elected governments continuously perpetrate atrocities against my people all over the world. And your support of them makes you directly responsible, just as I am directly responsible for protecting and avenging my Muslim brothers and sisters.'

In one important way, your argument matches that of the former Australian Prime Minister Malcolm Fraser. He says that we should 'no longer tolerate governments' that have fought the Iraq war, and you are telling the British people that they have the power, in a democracy, to get rid of their government. But your ethics and your action contradict each other. Fraser argues that we must support the human rights of those we abhor and despise. You decided to destroy and maim those that you abhorred and despised as you looked across at me in the Circle Line carriage that day.

You were right in some of your words in the video. Aspects of the media did 'try to put a spin on things to suit the government and to scare the masses into conforming to their power'. My own image – just like yours – on the front cover of the *Sun* newspaper, was used for that purpose. Yet it didn't succeed that time, and other British media took direct action, presenting my story against government anti-terror legislation, and focusing on spin as a threat to your and to my freedom.

There is a strong relationship between the second and third images of you that I am looking at. They represent the dialogue between two different identities. Most of us move between different identities, not least over major political events like the Iraq war. Important British novels like Ian McEwan's *Saturday* are powerful because they challenge in that dialogical way the faceless, too-busy everyday world where you and I briefly met one day in July. *Saturday* shows the way in which those different identities slide around, not just in our worlds of work and politics, but among the people we cherish most, who can so easily become 'terrorists' in their own context. One of your identities, the quiet listener in a classroom, I might have liked to meet. The other, the one that earlier was sitting in front of a bold, striped red and white carpet on a wall, I did meet, and don't ever want to meet again.

Others, I'm sure, will see something different in your eyes in my second image: eyes masking a malign purpose, deceitfully using deprived children to cover terrorist intent. Indeed, there are unconfirmed reports that you visited the 'mastermind' of Jemaah Islamiah, the group responsible for the Bali bombing, as early as 2001. But I don't hold with the simple theory that mastermind terrorists create cleanskin recruits. What research we have on terrorist psychology does not indicate they are noticeably different from other soldiers who die for a cause. I believe you chose to bomb that train not because you were a psychopath, but from a carefully considered decision in which your different identities and values were involved.

Research by the University of Chicago academic Richard Pape was quoted in the *Sydney Morning Herald* two days after 7 July, indicating that two-thirds of all suicide attacks by al-Qaeda were committed by people from countries where US troops were stationed. Pape says:

> The root cause of suicide terrorism is foreign occupation and the threat that foreign military presence poses to the local community's way of life. Hence any policy that seeks to conquer Muslim societies in order, deliberately, to transform their way of life is folly.

The Melbourne *Age* revealed on 18 July that research tended to confirm this. Both Saudi and Israeli security data on several hundred Iraq insurgents indicated that the vast majority were first-time terrorists, in Iraq 'to drive the infidels out of Arab land'. This Iraq does not represent just one 'Shock and Awe' invasion in March 2003. It symbolises many years of Western self-interested incursion into Muslim lands, which Ken Livingstone spoke publicly about in the week after your bombs, and you speak of as continuous atrocities against your people around the world.

And just three days after you exploded your bombs was the tenth anniversary of the slaughter of 10,000 men and boys by Bosnian Serb troops at Srebrenica. You are right, much of your brothers' blood has been spilled by and in the West over many years. In the *Sydney Morning Herald* a young Somali refugee was saying the same thing as you to journalist James Button at an east London mosque that week of the anniversary and your bombing:

> Why did you go into Iraq for the sake of human rights but leave people dying in Palestine? So, the bombs are bad, Muslims died too. This is a sad day. But somehow it is fair that the British see and feel what they do in Iraq every day.

Well, I saw and felt a little bit of what they do in Iraq every day. And I didn't go to the national memorial service for the dead and injured on 1 November 2005 because I didn't want any guilt that I felt absorbed and contained by state 'closure'. I don't need you to tell me that I am one of the affluent Western people replete with the 'tangible commodities that this world has to offer' whom you despised. Nor do I need to be told that what you call my democratically elected government (which by the way I didn't vote for) has been complicit in atrocities against your and other people in different parts of the world. And not just this particular government, but many others elected by their peoples over the past half century, as Pinter said in his Nobel speech. I don't accept the label of innocent victim that the media want to give to me, any more than I accept the label of mindless psychopath they give you. My British and Australian governments have taken that innocence away, and helped create more terrorists.

There are many people in Britain who feel the way I do. Some of the other victims of your attack on 7 July have said so publicly. They are all part of a powerful rhetorical force emerging out of a continuing, disempowered silence. This force challenges the treason laws and the sedition laws that our governments are using to silence and frighten people who, as Harold Pinter said at the end of his speech, want to restore what is so nearly lost to us: the dignity of humankind.

I agree with Pinter that despite the enormous odds we face, 'unflinching, unswerving, fierce intellectual determination, as citizens, to define the real truth of our lives and our societies is a crucial obligation' which we should all share. However, I also agree with Maggie and Erin and Craig when they apply their intelligence to deal yet again – and in a better way – with the everyday human problems arising from the terrorist world that left me lying at ground zero. That, too, is the determination of citizenship.

You could have been part of that citizenship, which I think you once thought hard about when you were a learning mentor in Beeston. Instead, you chose to kill us. That third image I have of you is not the way to another, better day.

Our words are never dead, Mohammad Sidique Khan, unless we stop speaking them.

Acknowledgements

This book is unusual in that many of the people one would normally acknowledge are walking through its pages and are acknowledged there directly or indirectly: the Erins, Maggies and Craigs, whom I pluralise here because they also represent many others who helped me via that wonderful combination of professional voice and personal support; and the more public figures, whom I refer to as public intellectuals or public communicators (in radio, television, the press, theatre, literature, art criticism) and whose voices, works and productions I have quoted directly as much as I can, because it is these that helped me think through my recovery, in ideas and emotions.

But there are others who did not walk onstage with me in the UK (which has been the recovery focus of this book). These include the closest of companions and friends in Australia: Jennifer and Sondi, Kerry and John, Joel and Anne, Wayne and Jennie, Mary and Julius, who, in their many emails and in personal thoughts sent quietly, helped me so very much; and thanks, too, to the professional colleagues in Australia and the US who emailed me supportively and, in the case of Warwick, my ARC co-researcher, helped to keep the Kosovo project alive through so many months of silence. My research colleagues in Kosovo and Norway, Willem, Dugi and Kenneth, were also supportive in exactly the right way. My family in Australia, Anton, Rowan and Marian, appear in this book only in their supportive 'strategic' roles, prescribed by Maggie and Erin. However they have their own tales to tell, of deep anxieties after 7/7, which I can only imagine as I wasn't there to share. I would like to thank the Australian Government for enabling visits to me of close family and whose representatives in Britain, Teresa from the Australian High Commission and Lou, a social worker with experience of earlier terrorist-induced calamities, were unfailing in their support to me and to my sons.

There are also many unnamed and (by me) unseen emergency workers who helped crucially on 7 July; there are the hospital doctors, surgeons, specialists, nurses and aids who looked after me so carefully and professionally after the explosion; the police from the bomb squad, shopkeepers, bank managers and media professionals who dealt with my problems sensitively – I owe a huge debt to all of them. I am very grateful, too, to colleagues and students from Brunel University and other universities, who visited me, emailed me and kept me (and the public) abreast of things in the months that followed when parts of the media were using my image in ways that, as one colleague emailed, 'you may not like'. Mary, the head of school's secretary at Brunel, is specially to be thanked for receiving and filtering endless phone calls from the media. Lindsay and Graham gave me another home in England – both in fact and in their thoughts – and I won't ever forget that.

Finally, there were my direct helpers in the writing of this book: Tim, whose idea it was, and who carried it through with intelligence and sympathy; Iain, an excellent copy editor who spent many hours with me in detailed debate over the intricacies of content and style; Charlie and Gerhard (with Gunhild) who came along and took some of the excellent shots in this book; and, above all, Janet, who not only helped me day by day throughout my recovery but was also a meticulous adviser and proofreader for the manuscript, and Anton, who as well as being my mentor (with Rowan) in engaging the media, showed superb professionalism in advising me with the manuscript. Thanks to all of you.

Index